Building Honor
in Academics

Building Honor in Academics

Case Studies in Academic Integrity

Valerie P. Denney
Camilla J. Roberts

JB JOSSEY-BASS™
A Wiley Brand

Published by John Wiley & Sons, Inc., Hoboken, New Jersey.
Published simultaneously in Canada.

For general information on our other products and services or for technical support, please contact our Customer Care Department within the United States at (800) 762-2974, outside the United States at (317) 572-3993 or fax (317) 572-4002.

If you believe you've found a mistake in this book, please bring it to our attention by emailing our reader support team at wileysupport@wiley.com with the subject line "Possible Book Errata Submission."

Wiley also publishes its books in a variety of electronic formats. Some content that appears in print may not be available in electronic formats. For more information about Wiley products, visit our web site at www.wiley.com.

Library of Congress Cataloging-in-Publication Data:

Names: Denney, Valerie, author. | Roberts, Camilla, author.
Title: Building honor in academics : case studies in academic integrity / Valerie Denney, Camilla Roberts.
Description: Hoboken, New Jersey : Jossey-Bass, 2023. | Includes bibliographical references and index.
Identifiers: LCCN 2022051892 (print) | LCCN 2022051893 (ebook) | ISBN 9781119880547 (paperback) | ISBN 9781119880554 (adobe pdf) | ISBN 9781119880561 (epub)
Subjects: LCSH: Education, Higher—Moral and ethical aspects—Case studies. | Cheating (Education)—Case studies.
Classification: LCC LB2324 .D46 2023 (print) | LCC LB2324 (ebook) | DDC 378.1/958—dc23/eng/20221207
LC record available at https://lccn.loc.gov/2022051892
LC ebook record available at https://lccn.loc.gov/2022051893

COVER DESIGN: PAUL MCCARTHY

Contents

Introduction   vii

Chapter 1   Honesty   1

Chapter 2   Trust   33

Chapter 3   Fairness   67

Chapter 4   Respect   99

Chapter 5   Responsibility   123

Chapter 6   Courage   153

Appendix A Alphabetical List of Case Studies Mapped
                to the Fundamental Values   181
Appendix B Alphabetical List of Case Studies Mapped
                to Audience   189
Appendix C Case Studies by Author   197
Appendix D Case Studies by Country of Origin   205
Index   215

Introduction

From the early beginnings of the Center for Academic Integrity, now the International Center for Academic Integrity (ICAI), the leadership and membership of the group strived to not only talk about or support academic integrity, but promote integrity and give institutions tools to create a culture of integrity on their own campuses. The Fundamental Values Project was designed to do just that.

According to Sally Cole, the center's first executive director from 1995 to 1999, the purpose of the original Fundamental Values was:

> . . . to identify and affirm the conditions under which student honesty would flourish. And we had the wisdom to recognize that it was an issue with campus climate that we were talking about. It was not just the student behavior but the environment/the settings in which a student decides to cheat or not to cheat. (Gallant, 2022)

After the work of Elizabeth Kiss, Jim Larimore, Gary Pavela, Don McCabe, Bill Kibler, Pat Drinan, Mary Olson, and Sally Cole, the first edition of the Fundamental Values was published in 1999 with the following five values: honesty, trust, fairness, respect and responsibility. In recognition of the Center's 20th anniversary in 2014, the document was reviewed in a second edition and the sixth value of courage was added. In 2021, a third edition was released, maintaining the same six values; however, attempting to connect the values to experiences global colleagues see daily at their institutions and with their students.

It is from this attempt to connect the values to the daily work that the idea of this case study book flourished. Leaders of ICAI saw a request and a need to be able to see examples of the fundamental values at work to help spur and continue conversations about academic integrity while also using these discussions as a training mechanism across the institution. We hope that the case studies found in *Building Honor in Academics*, organized by the six fundamental values of academic integrity, do just that. May they be talking points for a faculty meeting, training exercises for an honor council, or an ethical discussion in a classroom environment.

The mission of ICAI is to "cultivate integrity and academic communities throughout the world to promote ethical institutions and societies" and so throughout that mission the goal is to build the culture of academic integrity. We want to educate individuals; we want to educate our students; we want to educate our faculty. To have a commitment to academic integrity is to have a commitment to those values. We ask our students at our institutions to have these values, our faculty members to have these values, but also our institutions must maintain these values so our scholarly communities can flourish. *Building Honor in Academics* strives to help explore what it really means to live the fundamental values. The following is a description of the six fundamental values: honesty, trust, fairness, respect, responsibility, and courage.

Honesty

Honesty forms the indispensable foundation of integrity and is a prerequisite for full realization of trust, fairness, respect, and responsibility. Honesty can be seen as a prerequisite to realize all the other values. The ways we think about being honest is being truthful, giving credit to others, and promoting a culture in which we give credit to others. We keep our promises, and we provide factual evidence for our statements. Honesty is absolutely critical for both faculty and administrators model, not only in our words and what happens in our class in the classroom, but with our policies and procedures. In examining your policies and procedures, explore whether the policy encourages honesty, is learning centered, or encourages a student to be dishonest because it is more legalistic in its approach. We must examine our own situations to be able to answer how we encourage honesty; how we promote a culture of honesty; how we praise acts of honesty when we see them and make it something that's very much part of the value of the institution.

Trust

Trust is the ability to rely on the truth of someone or something. It is a fundamental pillar of academic pursuit. Within academics, we can promote trust by clearly stating our expectations and follow through on those expectations. That is whether we are faculty in the classroom and we are clearly stating the expectations for an assignment or if we are at the institution level where we are stating our expectations for academic integrity and what and how we will respond when breaches occur. Trust helps us promote transparency. Examples of trust in academia are to clearly state expectations, promote transparency, give credence, act with genuineness, and encourage mutual understanding. We want to trust others as we want to be trusted ourselves. We hold each other accountable to trust one another and encourage each other with a mutual understanding and act with genuineness when we have trust.

Fairness

Fairness is focusing on impartial treatment or looking at bias making sure you understand where your biases are associated with this fair or impartial treatment. Fairness emphasizes and reinforces those values of truth within logic and rationality. Fairness can be seen by making sure that the ideas of the rules, policies, and procedures are applied consistently as it applies both to the institution, faculty member, and student. Engaging with others equitably ensures you keep an open mind, taking responsibility for your own actions. A faculty leads by example making sure to uphold those principles associated with the fairness principle and to communicate those expectations as we go through the academic year making sure that the institution has clear, useful, and consistent policies and that there is a degree of transparency.

Respect

Respect in academic communities is reciprocal and requires showing respect for oneself as well. Examples of respect include receiving feedback willingly, practicing active listening, showing empathy, seeking open communication, affirming others, and recognizing the consequences of our word and actions on others. It is not just that it is expecting trust from others but you also want to make sure that it is respectful, which shows that this trust goes both ways. To be clear, this is not only between individuals or between an individual and an institution, but one's self as well—respecting oneself. This can of course be completed in many different ways. As educators, we want students to have an active role in contributing to discussion and it means at times there are going to be some discussions where not everybody is going to agree. Faculty need to recognize students as individuals and to take seriously the ideas that those students have, respectfully. Respect is also having the faculty give full honest feedback and actionable feedback. Within respect in the institution, we must embrace that it is healthy to have some spirited discussions. The respect shown among the discussions gives the ability for individuals to have those disagreements but also to be able to proceed forward and to express their views.

Responsibility

Responsibility identifies that upholding the values of integrity is simultaneously an individual duty and a shared concern. Examples of responsibility in academic life include engaging in difficult conversations, knowing and following institutional rules and policies, holding yourself accountable for your actions, following through with tasks and expectations, and modeling good behavior. It is the idea of making sure that one is holding oneself accountable for their own actions. We also often want our students to take responsibility for their actions. To demonstrate this responsibility, we encourage all at the institution to first know the policies, but then to take responsibility to ask for clarification if needed. Responsibility is also creating understanding and respecting personal boundaries and following through. Just as students should take responsibility for the work they submit; faculty members are responsible for teaching our students and holding our students accountable. The faculty should also take responsibility for when things do not go quite as well as they planned with an assignment or maybe they were not quite as clear on their assignment guidelines. We also ask our institutions to take responsibility possibly through a long-term 5- or 10-year plan. These long-term plans allow for transparency of both successes and failures.

Courage

Courage differs from the preceding fundamental values by being more a quality or capacity of character. However, as with each of the values, courage can be practiced and developed. Courage often is interpreted as a lack of fear. In reality, courage is the capacity to act in accordance with one's values despite fear. Examples of courage include being brave when others might not, taking a stand to address wrongdoing, being willing to take risk and risk failure, and being undaunted in defending integrity. One might need courage to be able to act in accordance with the other values. The previous five values sometimes can be intimidating, and one must have the courage to live out the value. For a student to speak up to their peers takes quite a bit of courage, or for our faculty members (especially prior to tenure) to stand up for what they think or what they believe in takes courage. We encourage all to have that voice to be able to take a stand, address wrongdoing, and understand there might be some discomfort but if you are standing up for the good, for something that you believe in, then it is worth it in the end. We ask our institutions to have courage just to make statements against wrongdoing. We have seen numerous current societal issues, and we encourage our institutions to take a stand to describe the culture and the community wanted at the institution. The courage in turn will continue to develop those previous five fundamental values. The six values will then lead to a high level of academic integrity culture at the institution.

Structure of the Book

Building Honor in Academics: Case Studies in Academic Integrity is made up of 67 case studies written by authors from eleven different countries (United States, Canada, Australia, Germany, Indonesia, Latvia, Mexico, Nigeria, Puerto Rico, Switzerland, and the United Kingdom). The cases are organized into six chapters based upon the primary fundamental value the case entails. Many cases also have secondary values as well. Authors of the cases also directed their case toward a specific audience: faculty, staff, academic integrity office, researcher, or administration/other. Each case study follows a similar format beginning with a summary of the case, supporting information, a discussion of the values associated with the case, guiding questions and a conclusion.

To assist in the use of this case study book, the appendices have organized the cases in various topics.

- Appendix A is an alphabetical listing of the case studies mapped to the primary fundamental value.
- Appendix B is an alphabetical listing of the case studies mapped to the targeted audience of the case.
- Appendix C is a listing of case studies by author's name.
- Appendix D is a list of case studies by country of origin.

Reference

Gallant, Tricia Bertram. "It Takes a Village": The Origins of the International Center for Academic Integrity." International Center for Academic Integrity, 2022. https://academicintegrity.org/images/conference/It_Takes_a_Village.pdf

Chapter 1
Honesty

Chapter Contents:

Buyers' Remorse
  Loretta Frankovitch, University at Buffalo, United States
Investment Pains
  Sara Kellogg, Iowa State University, United States
Professor Purposely Publishes Student Paper Without Giving Credit
  Martin Daumiller, University of Augsburg, Germany
Photoshop: The Easiest (Worst!) Way Out
  Lucila María Puente Cruz, Dulce Abril Castro Escalón, and Daniela Gallego Salazar,
  Tecnológico de Monterrey, México
Should I Pay the Contract Cheating Sites to Get the Answer?
  Ann Liang, University of Saskatchewan, Canada
Readied Recalcitrance
  Christian Moriarty, St. Petersburg College, United States
Where's Waldo: IP Address Incongruence and Student Surrogacy
  Aaron Glassman, Cheryl Lentz, and Denise Bollenback, Embry-Riddle Aeronautical
  University, United States
Foiling Attempts to Facilitate File Sharing: Updating Assessment
  Ann M. Rogerson and Oriana Milani Price, University of Wollongong, Australia
Caught in the Act
  Tay McEdwards, Oregon State University, United States
To Burn Bridges or to Build Them?
  Blaire N. Wilson and Jason T. Ciejka, Emory University, United States
A Syllabus Sleight of Hand
  Jason T. Ciejka and Blaire N. Wilson, Emory University, United States

Honesty forms the indispensable foundation of integrity and is a prerequisite for full realization of trust, fairness, respect, and responsibility. The ways we think about being honest is being truthful, giving credit to others, and promoting a culture in which we give credit to others. We keep our promises, and we provide factual evidence for our statements. Honesty is absolutely critical for both faculty and administrators model, not only in our words and what happens in our class in the classroom, but with our policies and procedures. In examining your policies and procedures, explore whether the policy encourages honesty, is learning centered, or encourages a student to be dishonest because it is more legalistic in its approach. We must examine our own situations to be able to answer how we encourage honesty; how we promote a culture of honesty; how we praise acts of honesty when we see them and make it something that's very much part of the value of the institution.

There are 11 case studies in this book which address the primary value of honesty.

Case Studies Focused on the Student. There are four case studies which primarily address the student perspective.

Two of the cases address unauthorized collaboration and/or use of resources. In "Case 1: *Buyers' Remorse*" two students purchase an online assignment, but don't actually use it to solve their homework problems. Nevertheless, they receive a bill from the online tutor which they don't pay, causing the tutor to turn them in to the faculty member.

In "Case 2: *Investment Pains*" a faculty member at a university finds similar homework submissions for two students including the same document. One student said she simply used a peer's laptop since hers was broken but denies misconduct.

One of the cases addresses giving proper credit. In "Case 3: *Professor Purposely Publishes Student Paper Without Giving Credit*" a student in her final year as an undergraduate conducted a research project independently in a term paper. A few years later, the student discovered an article written by her former professor that was nearly identical to her former term paper, but without attributing the work to the student.

The final case also deals with deception. In "Case 4: *Photoshop: The Easiest (Worst!) Way Out*" a student studied abroad and took two courses but failed one. She used Photoshop to change the failing grade into a passing grade on the transcript and submitted it to her home university.

Case Studies Focused on the Faculty and/or Administrator. There are seven case studies which primarily address actual or potential unauthorized collaboration and/or use of resources. In "Case 5: *Should I Pay the Contract Cheating Sites to Get the Answer*," an accounting instructor notices that several students in her class have answered questions incorrectly using a method that she did not teach. The instructor found the exam questions on a contract cheating site where a tutor has provided the answer that is only viewable for a fee. The instructor contemplates paying for the proof of misconduct.

In "Case 6: *Readied Recalcitrance*," a student turns in a paper that shows 65 percent similarity to a paper with another student's name on it and on a paper-sharing website. The student denies the allegations.

In "Case 7: *Where's Waldo: IP Address Incongruence and Student Surrogacy*," a faculty member noticed that some students had different IP addresses when submitting their weekly discussion posts than when submitting their heavily weighted activities like research papers. The faculty decided to investigate the complexities of this dilemma by examining the log data.

In "Case 8: *Foiling Attempts to Facilitate File Sharing: Updating Assessment*," a faculty member notices that the assessment tasks had not been routinely updated and lacked model answer examples. The faculty member has heard that students were uploading answers from past courses to file sharing sites, and she wants to proactively address this situation.

In the final case about unauthorized resources "Case 9: *Caught in the Act*" a testing assistant routinely assists faculty with concerns about online exams that require proctoring. While reviewing a video of an exam session proctored by a third-party online proctoring vendor, the testing assistant noticed that before the exam started the screen share captured an open Excel spreadsheet with thousands of entries about student information and appeared to be used for organized contract cheating.

One case addresses providing proper credit. In "Case 10: *To Burn Bridges or to Build Them?*" a staff member proposes a solution to a staffing problem in the office during a team meeting. The solution is implemented successfully and praised by the senior leadership for providing an innovative solution. However, the staff member learned this idea from a colleague, and she has not been given credit.

The final case study "Case 11: *A Syllabus Sleight of Hand*" deals with yet another form of deception. In this case, a faculty member is designing a syllabus for a new course that will be reviewed by the university's curriculum committee. The faculty adds several assignments to the proposed syllabus that will meet the new standards, but he has no intention of following through on these once the course is approved.

In addition to the 11 case studies in this chapter on honesty, 23 other case studies in this book address honesty as a secondary value. Refer to that value chapter as shown for an introduction to each case study.

Trust:

- *Where in the Metaverse Is Boris' Voice?*
- *Suspicious Success*
- *My Students, My Research Subjects—Trust in Faculty, Researcher, and Student Relationships*
- *But They'll Never Know*
- *Machine Learning: Trusting the Training Data, or the Trainer?*
- *Capturing the Impostor Syndrome Through Turnitin*

Fairness:

- *Collusion Confusion*
- *Higher Learning, Higher Stakes*
- *All for One and One for All*

Respect:

- *Time Is a Non-Renewable Resource*
- *Email Déjà Vu*
- *Respect and Honor Through Intentional Proactive Student Actions*

Responsibility:

- *Posting Faulty Information to Bait Students*
- *Does Co-Authorship Imply a Responsibility for the Whole Document?*
- *Alma Mater Should Always Matter*
- *Student's Legal Defense and Institutional Responsibility*
- *Contract Cheating Coercion*

Courage:

- *Mock Police Board Exam Puts Students in the Hot Seat*
- *Taking a Stand for Integrity: A Whistleblower's Tale*
- *The Blackmail Blues*
- *To Tell or Not to Tell: That Is the Question*
- *Self-Plagiarism in PhD Student's Thesis*
- *The Handy Dandy Dictionary*

Case 1: Buyers' Remorse

Loretta Frankovitch, University at Buffalo, United States

Synopsis/Summary

Two students purchase an online assignment, but don't actually use it to solve their homework problems. Nevertheless, they receive a bill from the online tutor which they don't pay, causing the tutor to turn them in to the faculty member. The instructor must then determine if and how to sanction them.

Supporting Information

James and Joe, two undergraduate computer science students, don't understand their computer science homework. It is after hours, so they cannot contact their professor or TA. Desperate, and running out of time, they purchase a solution from Tariq, an online tutor on a "help" website.

While waiting for the solution, James and Joe have second thoughts. They also realize that they can complete the majority of the project on their own. They do so, and submit it prior to the assignment deadline and prior to receiving anything from Tariq.

A little later, the completed assignment and a bill arrive from the online tutor. Since the students have already turned in their assignment, they don't pay the bill.

The online tutor has given them several days to pay, but because they don't, he contacts their professor, Dr. Baker, showing the students' request and the completed assignment.

Upon comparison of the submitted assignment and the "purchased" assignment, Dr. Baker determines that the students did not use the "purchased" assignment in their homework submission. However, at their next class meeting, Dr. Baker asks James and Joe to stay afterward to discuss a possible breach in academic integrity.

DR. BAKER:	Gentleman—did you purchase your last project from an online tutor?
JAMES:	Actually, yes . . . , but we didn't use it.

JOE: We didn't have to. We thought we didn't have enough time to finish it, but as we waited for the tutor to complete the assignment, we ended up figuring it out ourselves.

DR. BAKER: After looking at your submission, it doesn't bear resemblance to the "purchased" assignment, so I'm inclined to believe you, but why didn't you pay the online tutor?

JAMES: We really didn't use his work, so we didn't feel we needed to pay him.

Value Discussion

The primary value in this case study is honesty. According to the ICAI Fundamental Values document (https://academicintegrity.org/resources/fundamental-values), honesty requires truthfulness. In this sense, the students appear to have complied by answering their faculty member truthfully. But honesty also means that you will keep promises, a rule that the students break at least twice. First, they break a promise with the faculty member to abide by the rules and policies of the course and complete their work honestly, and second, they break a promise with the online tutor to exchange an assignment for money.

A secondary value seen is responsibility. Dr. Baker bears responsibility for teaching his students certain concepts and assessing what they know. He cannot uphold this responsibility if the students do not complete their work with honesty. His responsibility to the institution and to his profession is broken if he allows the students to violate the policies. The students bear responsibility to the faculty member, the institution, themselves, and anyone with whom they've entered an agreement, even if that promise is predicated on dishonesty. Two wrongs do not make a right. They need to adhere to course and university policies, and "model good behavior" (ICAI, 2021), neither of which they have done.

Another secondary value evident in this scenario is courage. The students had the courage to complete their assignment and turn it in without waiting to compare it to or check it against the tutor's answers. And, more importantly, they had the courage to respond to their professor with the truth. They could have lied to Dr. Baker in an attempt to cover their dishonest actions, but they chose to admit their mistake and possibly face negative consequences. According to ICAI's fundamental values, courage in academic settings may "include opportunities to make choices, learn from them, and grow" (ICAI, 2021). James and Joe made a poor choice, but learned from it, both academically and personally, result-ing in a more honest and courageous choice to tell Dr. Baker the truth about the whole situation.

Question Discussion

1. Is poor behavior a reason to charge students with an academic integrity violation, even if the purchased assignment was ulti-mately not used?
2. Is it unethical that these students didn't pay their online tutor? Or doesn't the tutor deserve to be paid since he was operating unethically?
3. What is the faculty's responsibility in all this? Should they give the students a lesser charge than someone else who actually carried through with contract cheating?

Conclusion

Students often make errors in judgment, but eventually come to an honest and responsible decision on their own.

Reference

International Center for Academic Integrity [ICAI]. The Fundamental Values of Academic Integrity, 3rd ed., 2021. http://www.academicintegrity.org/the-fundamental-values-of-academic-integrity.

Case 2: Investment Pains

Sara Kellogg, Iowa State University, United States

Synopsis/Summary

Faculty at an American accredited university find similar home-work submissions for Tan and Lu. Faculty find the same author for both spreadsheets in document properties and refer the case to the student conduct office for cheating. Lu informs the student conduct office that because her laptop is broken, she had used Tan's to complete course-work, but denies misconduct. Faculty disagree with the conduct office's finding of non-responsibility for academic misconduct and proceed to review all prior homework submissions.

Supporting Information

Tan and Lu are roommates enrolled in a Business Management course, and both received an email from their faculty, Dr. Rose, regarding their most recent homework assignment. Dr. Rose found a few similarities in Tan and Lu's spreadsheets, and upon closer inspection, discovered the same author in the properties of both documents. Dr. Rose already had some concerns about these students as they've missed a number of the same class periods and are currently earning very similar grades in the course. Dr. Rose informs the students they have been referred to the student conduct office for academic misconduct, and they will both receive a zero if responsible. During their meetings with student conduct, the students are asked to explain the same author on their spreadsheets.

Lu shares, "My laptop broke around midterms, so I've been using Tan's laptop for all my coursework, which is why we had the same document author, but I didn't cheat." Tan shares a similar account, adding, "We had some similarities because we study together, but a lot of our formulas and work were different. I don't understand why Dr. Rose isn't paying attention to that." After review, the student conduct office determines there is not a preponderance of evidence to support that academic misconduct occurred and notifies the faculty. The students were found not responsible. Dr. Rose strongly disagrees with this finding and believes the students have gotten away with cheating, so decides to pull up all their previous homework and exams to compare more closely, looking for evidence to support his suspicion.

Value Discussion

Honesty is the primary value in this case. Students are expected to be honest in their coursework and engagement with faculty and may be asked to support their account when there are reasons for suspicion. Faculty may have questions about a student's honesty and still facilitate an equitable classroom experience. An integrity office may have to make decisions in support of a student's account as supported by the relevant and available evidence, regardless of suspicions of dishonesty.

A secondary value in this case is responsibility. Students have the responsibility to communicate issues that may arise or create suspicion about their work and do this proactively when possible. Faculty have a responsibility to ensure equitable treatment of students, and additional responsibility not to harbor resentment or seek reprisal for unfounded suspicions of academic dishonesty. Integrity offices have a responsibility to review and weigh all relevant information in making thoughtful and well-informed decisions.

Question Discussion

1. Should the students in this situation have taken some type of steps to proactively prevent this referral?
2. Is it possible for a faculty's perception of a student's investment in their course to influence their suspicion of academic misconduct?
3. When a faculty disagrees or is frustrated with a decision by a student conduct office related to a referral for academic misconduct, what options do they have for response?
4. What are some strategies an integrity office might use to reduce frustration from faculty in a case where students are found not responsible?
5. What is the appropriate action or outcome if the faculty does find issues with prior coursework submissions from these students?

Conclusion

Honesty is the foundation for trust in the classroom, and even when challenging, faculty may have to accept a student's account to provide a fair and objective learning environment.

Case 3: Professor Purposely Publishes Student Paper Without Giving Credit

Martin Daumiller, University of Augsburg, Germany

Synopsis/Summary

In her final year as an undergraduate student at a large university in the US, Janine conducted a research project independently and described her findings in a term paper. Her professor praised her paper and graded it with an A. Having started her graduate studies at another university,

Janine continued with further research on this topic. She discovered an article written by her former professor that was recently published and was nearly identical to her former term paper; the professor even kept the exact text that Janine wrote in many instances.

Supporting Information

As soon as Janine read the article, she called her friend, Maggy.

JANINE: Hi Maggy! Do you remember the term paper I wrote in my final year? I just came across the exact same paper, but allegedly written by my former professor, Prof. Umbridge. It just got published!

MAGGY: Wow, so Prof. Umbridge built on aspects of your work?

JANINE: No! It's the exact same paper. Only a few words are different. Other than that, it's identical!

MAGGY: Wow—I'm shocked. You put so much work and effort into that paper. Did she at least give you credit?

JANINE: No! Nothing. Not even a mention in the acknowledgements. I don't know what to do! This is so unfair, and I feel so exploited. What do you think I should do?

MAGGY: Do you still have all the data on your laptop? Everything that refers to that project?

JANINE: Yes! I even have the comments Prof. Umbridge made to the article in the first stages of writing the paper.

MAGGY: Perfect, that's all we need! Does your former university have an academic integrity office? I recommend that you go there first thing tomorrow. Maybe they can even help to take the article down! Good luck!

JANINE: Thank you for your advice. I'll keep you updated!

Value Discussion

Honesty, the primary value in this case study, is the fundamental premise of academia and forms a scaffold around scientific actions and beliefs. The scientific process entails gathering new and authentic findings for a deeper and better understanding of nature. Researchers should act with honesty and integrity, in best knowledge and with full conscience throughout all stages of their profession, including the publication process. This makes them and their research findings trustworthy and reliable. Faculty members should therefore always give credit to the owner of the work, model exemplary behavior, and follow academic rules.

Responsibility, a secondary value in the case, not only entails being a good teacher when working as a professor or researcher, but also shouldering academic responsibility. The role of a professor involves being an experienced contact who is trustworthy and reachable so that students can learn and mimic exemplary scientific behavior. Professors are seen as role models by many, within and beyond the respective institution. In such a position, scientific principles should be advocated out of personal conviction. Not giving credit where it is due breaches the principles of scientific work and leads to a loss of credibility.

Question Discussion

1. What ethical standards are breached when submitting students' papers for publication?
2. Beyond going to an academic integrity office: What other options does Janine have to move forward? How can she be supported in that way?
3. What can the university administration do to avoid such cases in the future?
4. Should there be work-related consequences for the professor? If yes, what seems to be adequate?

Conclusion

Scientific credibility is based on honesty where no exceptions should be tolerated. All members, particularly professors, should have this conviction and convey it to the outside.

Case 4: Photoshop: The Easiest (Worst!) Way Out

Lucila María Puente Cruz, Dulce Abril Castro Escalón, and Daniela Gallego Salazar, Tecnológico de Monterrey, Mexico

Synopsis/Summary

Sarah Lopez studied abroad for a semester in Royal University. She studied two courses but failed one. Therefore, she took the transcript provided by the Royal University, used Photoshop to change the failing grade into a passing grade and submitted it to Mount College, her home university. However, Alan Castro, the administrator in charge of the transcript process, received the transcript from Royal University and confirmed the failing grade. In consequence, he reported this situation to the Academic Integrity Committee.

Supporting Information

Sarah Lopez studied abroad for a semester in Royal University as an exchange student. It was the first time she was far away from home, and did not know anybody there; consequently, besides studying, she decided to take this experience as an opportunity to get to know the city and make new friends. Sarah was doing great with the Business Strategy course, and was confident of her learning, since it was a subject she had always felt passionate about. However, as the semester went by, and became busier with her social commitments, she started to feel a lot of pressure studying the Global Economics course, which she certainly had trouble understanding since the beginning of the academic period.

Sarah looked for academic counseling in Royal University, but it was too late. She found out she had failed the course and video-called a close friend back in Mexico to ask for advice. Sarah said to her friend, "I do not know how I get to this point of failing this course. I am willing to do anything to fix this! My family and I cannot afford another semester." Worried that she would not be able to continue her studies with a failed course, Sarah took the transcript provided by Royal University, used Photoshop to change the failing grade into a passing grade, and submitted it to her home university once she was back in Mexico. A few weeks later, Alan Castro, the administrator in charge of the transcript process in Mount College, found out that Sarah had forged an official document and committed academic dishonesty. Despite being dubious of what to do because it crossed his mind this misconduct could be considered a violation of the law, he decided to report the situation to the Academic Integrity Office and notified Sarah.

Value Discussion

The primary value in this case is honesty. Sarah was desperate to obtain a passing grade that she focused on doing whatever it took to obtain the results she hoped for rather than being honest to herself, her family, and her home university. The Fundamental Values of Academic Integrity (2021) state that "honesty begins with individuals and extends out into the larger community." This means that students "must be honest with themselves and with each other." Sarah decided not to be truthful to herself and provided forged evidence to her home university, instead of accepting the fact that she had failed the course, and dealt with the consequences.

Trust is a secondary value. "Trust is the ability to rely on the truth of someone or something" (ICAI, 2021), and it is a necessary foundation of academic work. Students and faculty are required to build trust by being honest and honoring mutual commitments. Sarah did not act with genuineness and transparency, both necessary traits to foster and maintain trust. When trust is infringed, there must be consequences that ensure that academic standards are being protected.

Another secondary value in this case is respect. In this case study, Sarah did not respect the institution's rules regarding academic integrity, but Alan Castro did. He showed the value of respect when he followed the academic integrity regulations and procedures of Mount College, and reported the academic dishonesty committed by Sarah. Respect is required "to tackle challenges without compromising your own values," and it is necessary for "scholarly communities to succeed" (Fundamental Values of Academic Integrity, 2021).

A final secondary value is courage. In this case, Alan had the courage to do the right thing. He followed the rules of academic integrity of the institution, took a stand to address the situation, and reported Sarah to the Academic Integrity Office, despite the outcome. According to the Fundamental Values of Academic Integrity (2021), "courage is the capacity to act in accordance with one's values despite fear," and Alan had the courage to "hold himself, students, and other faculty accountable for maintaining a culture of integrity."

Question Discussion

1. Should Alan Castro, the administrator in charge of the transcript process, talk to Sarah about the situation? Or should he just report the academic dishonesty issue and make sure the correct grade is applied?

2. What are the key pieces of information the administrative staff of a university must have in terms of academic integrity?
3. Does Alan Castro have to inform Royal University about the academic misconduct committed by Sarah?

Conclusion

Academic integrity is built on the integrity of the degrees and official documentation of a university. Failure to have honesty on those lead to a failure of a culture of integrity.

Reference

International Center for Academic Integrity [ICAI]. The Fundamental Values of Academic Integrity, 3rd ed., 2021. https://academicintegrity.org/images/pdfs/20019_ICAI-Fundamental-Values_R12.pdf

Case 5: Should I Pay the Contract Cheating Sites to Get the Answer?

Ann Liang, University of Saskatchewan, Canada

Synopsis/Summary

Susan is an accounting instructor in a business college in Canada. While grading an online midterm, she notices that several students in her class have answered questions incorrectly using a method that she did not teach. Susan searches online for her exam questions and finds them on a contract cheating site where a tutor has provided the answer that is only viewable for a fee. Susan is unsure how to proceed and contemplates paying for the proof of misconduct.

Supporting Information

Susan finds that the accounting midterm questions have been posted on a contract cheating site and had been answered by the service during the time that students were taking their online exam. The answers for the questions were incorrect and done in a method that was not taught in class. Susan had over 50 students with the same incorrect answer and surmised that they must have texted the answers to each other. She has not spoken with the students yet.

With so many suspected students involved Susan is afraid to tell the dean of the college about the situation without proof as she is new to teaching, and afraid she might be seen as a "bad teacher." However, the only way to see the answer is to pay a fee to access the site. Susan feels uneasy about paying for access. With a bit more digging, Susan finds frequently asked questions on the site about filing an academic misconduct claim and question take down request, but the process seems long and complicated. Susan is also unsure how to approach talking to the group of students that she suspects of cheating. The entire situation is overwhelming, and Susan just contemplates paying for the proof of misconduct to end the situation easily and quickly.

Value Discussion

The primary value in this case is honesty. Honesty is at the core of integrity, and there are multiple instances where honesty would help Susan resolve this situation. Susan should be honest with her dean regarding the situation. Susan should also demonstrate honesty to her own students but letting them know what she's found and what she expects from students who might have participated in this, instead of using a dishonest method of gathering evidence such as purchasing the answer for the sole purpose of catching cheaters.

A secondary value in this case is fairness which indicates impartial treatment and is crucial in approaching academic integrity cases. Faculty are quick to jump to an assumption of guilt and punishment instead of innocence until proven guilty. Susan here did not even see the answer from the website and did not speak to the students before creating a scenario and assuming guilt. To help with fairness, following an institution's rules and policies regarding academic integrity cases can help guide how faculty respond to students with an open mind.

Responsibility is a final secondary value in this case. Susan as a faculty member has a responsibility to uphold the values of integrity and the integrity of the program by modeling what responsible behavior looks like. If Susan chose to pay for the answer, she would still have to be accountable for her actions, which could have consequences depending on the institution's policies and procedures for how to handle misconduct cases. Susan can be responsible by having those difficult conversations with the dean and the accused students while following institutional rules and procedures.

Question Discussion

1. How can Susan find proof without paying into this website?
2. What's the best way for Susan to approach talking to so many students who possibly colluded?
3. What can Susan do in the future to prevent answer purchasing and sharing from happening?
4. What can the institution do to support new faculty with academic misconduct cases?

Conclusion

An instructor must model honesty to uphold the integrity of their program and to ensure that academic integrity cases are dealt with fairly.

Case 6: Readied Recalcitrance

Christian Moriarty, St. Petersburg College, United States

Synopsis/Summary

A student turns in a paper that shows 65 percent similarity. It is patently clear they did not write the majority of the paper, as the thesis and most of the supporting ideas are taken from a paper found in the similarity checker database with another student's name on it and on a paper-sharing website. When contacted, the student swears up and down they wrote it themselves and will not budge from the position.

Supporting Information

Miranda Alenko, a professor, assigned her students a paper analyzing a work from a famous psychologist. The work is well-trodden in academic circles and is useful for students to go over as training for deeper thought into the field.

Professor Alenko received a paper from a student, Kasumi Vega, that immediately came up on the similarity checker software as 65 percent similar to other sources. The software notes multiple sentences in a row, multiple times throughout, as pulled from elsewhere. Kasumi's name is there, and some things have been moved around, but it is clear she did not write this. The ideas and many of the sentences come from a specific paper, with another student's name, written at another university a few years ago. Digging deeper, Professor Alenko also finds this paper on an infamous paper-sharing (read: cheating) site on the internet. There are citations, but some of those citations also appear in the other papers, and quotation marks are not used on lifted material. Alenko believes the student clearly substantially plagiarized the paper.

Alenko crafted a carefully written email comparing Kasumi's paper to the ones found elsewhere, including highlighting substantially the same language and ideas. Kasumi immediately responded writing that she did not cheat, had no intention of cheating, and seemed offended at the very mention of it.

Value Discussion

One of the primary tenants of honesty in the academic integrity space is that a paper with your name on it means you wrote it. Plagiarism is dishonest. Of course, it is important to consider that the student may be honest here; they said they don't think they cheated; maybe they don't know what cheating or plagiarism is! Or at the very least is not familiar with the nuances of what extent is considered original writing and what is plagiarism.

Fairness is one of the secondary values addressed in this case study. When considering sanctions for students that have cheated, fairness demands that intent and knowledge of plagiarism expectations is considered. Many students genuinely do not understand plagiarism or the expectations of original academic writing. This can be from any number of reasons, including lack of formal instruction in the topic, non-western education, or non-traditional students that have not been in a formal education setting for some time and even if they do, the extent of the plagiarism and its harm should be taken into account.

The final secondary value addressed in this case study is responsibility. Despite a lack of intent, genuine, good-faith mistakes, or harried patch writing under deadline, students need to take responsibility for plagiarism they commit. Even with the excuse or reasons of ignorance or time pressure, the standards of academic writing hold and they are expected to be abided by. And it is the responsibility of educators to instruct students in appropriate writing strategies to prevent plagiarism or learn from their mistakes so that students may learn from them.

Question Discussion

1. As a faculty member, how can you approach a student who is denying charges of plagiarism?
2. What are the appropriate follow-ups and/or remedial steps for such a student? How can a student take appropriate responsibility for their actions? What sanctions would be fair in this case?

Conclusion

Whether a purposeful strategy to avoid repercussions or a genuine ignorance of plagiarism, it is important to discuss with accused students to educate them and not unnecessarily punish them.

Case 7: Where's Waldo: IP Address Incongruence and Student Surrogacy

Aaron Glassman, Cheryl Lentz, and Denise Bollenback, Embry-Riddle Aeronautical University, United States

Synopsis/Summary

Jane is a faculty member in the College of Business and Technology at a university in the United States. In grading papers one afternoon, Jane noticed an interesting anomaly. Some students had different IP addresses for submitting their weekly discussion posts than when submitting their heavily weighted activities like research papers. Jane decided to investigate further and discovered a concerning pattern in the learning management system (LMS) logs.

Supporting Information

In taking a deeper dive, Jane asks: "Why are there two logins in two very different locations when this student submits their assignments?"

She discovered that a student who lived in Florida had a Florida IP address during the week, but a different IP address that was from India when their papers were submitted. This student seemed to be having help by an unknown source since after the submission from an Indian IP address, a Florida IP address would review that same submission within the hour and download the submission.

This pattern suggests that someone else logs in under the student's account to submit papers not written by this student, a surrogate likely emails the student saying, "I submitted your paper" and then the student logs in thereafter to ensure paper submission; the logs show the student downloads a copy of the submitted paper for their records. This student surrogate could also attend classes by contributing to the weekly discussion on behalf of the student. If the student gave their password to a third party, that third party could attend school as a surrogate for the student. With information technology (IT) support, it was determined that the student approved the two-factor authentication logins to where the requested login access was from an India-based IP address and the two-factor approval from a Florida-based IP address. Table A is an illustration of domestic surrogacy and Table B is an illustration of international surrogacy both based on IP address translation.

Table A   Example LMS log showing a student hired another student at a different university to login and complete their work (domestic surrogacy). Specific IP addresses and more detailed LMS data was removed to protect privacy. Items in red generate a pattern and are flagged by the time/distance algorithm as possible surrogate activity.

Lms Activity Code	Date/Time (Zulu)	Ip Address Translation
Assignments	2016-11-10T04:26:27Z	United States – Rochester, – NY Frontier Communications of America, Inc
Assignments	2016-11-04T01:50:34Z	United States – Rochester, – NY Frontier Communications of America, Inc.
Assignments	2016-10-26T20:17:28Z	United States – West Lafayette, – IN Purdue University – Purdue University
submissions/ downloads	2016-10-20T13:23:56Z	United States – West Lafayette, – IN Purdue University – Purdue University

(Continued)

Table A   (Continued)

Lms Activity Code	Date/Time (Zulu)	Ip Address Translation
submissions/ previews	2016-10-20T13:23:53Z	United States – West Lafayette, – IN Purdue University – Purdue University
Submissions	2016-10-20T13:23:53Z	United States – West Lafayette, – IN Purdue University – Purdue University
Assignments	2016-10-12T00:25:20Z	United States – West Lafayette, – IN Purdue University – Purdue University
Submissions	2016-10-12T00:25:20Z	United States – West Lafayette, – IN Purdue University – Purdue University
Assignments	2016-10-12T00:25:06Z	United States – West Lafayette, – IN Purdue University – Purdue University
Assignments	2016-10-11T22:09:01Z	United States – West Lafayette, – IN Purdue University – Purdue University
submissions/ previews	2016-10-11T22:08:51Z	United States – West Lafayette, – IN Purdue University – Purdue University
Submissions	2016-10-11T22:08:50Z	United States – West Lafayette, – IN Purdue University – Purdue University
Assignments	2016-10-09T02:15:46Z	United States – Mt Laurel, – NJ Comcast Cable Communications, LLC
Assignments	2016-10-05T21:29:31Z	United States – Los Angeles, – CA HugeServer Networks, LLC – HugeServer Networks, LLC
submissions/ downloads	2016-10-05T21:07:44Z	United States – West Lafayette, – IN Purdue University – Purdue University
Assignments	2016-10-05T21:07:37Z	United States – West Lafayette, – IN Purdue University – Purdue University
Submissions	2016-10-05T21:07:37Z	United States – West Lafayette, – IN Purdue University – Purdue University
Assignments	2016-10-05T21:07:24Z	United States – West Lafayette, – IN Purdue University – Purdue University
Assignments	2016-10-05T19:33:52Z	United States – West Lafayette, – IN Purdue University – Purdue University
submissions/ previews	2016-10-05T19:33:42Z	United States – West Lafayette, – IN Purdue University – Purdue University
Assignments	2016-09-30T14:20:39Z	United States – West Lafayette, – IN Purdue University – Purdue University
Assignments	2016-09-30T00:57:13Z	United States – Los Angeles, – CA HugeServer Networks, LLC
Assignments	2016-09-30T00:42:51Z	United States – Los Angeles, – CA HugeServer Networks, LLC

Table B Example LMS log showing a student hired a company located in another country to login and complete their work (international surrogacy). Specific IP addresses and more detailed LMS data was removed to protect privacy. Items in red generate a pattern and are flagged by the time/distance algorithm as possible surrogate activity.

Lms Activity Code	Date/Time (Zulu)	Ip Address Translation
Assignments	2016-11-21T03:41:16Z	Kenya – Ebene, – Unknown African Network Information Center – Airtel Broadband
submissions/ previews	2016-11-21T03:40:23Z	Kenya – Ebene, – Unknown African Network Information Center – Airtel Broadband
Submissions	2016-11-21T03:40:21Z	Kenya – Ebene, – Unknown African Network Information Center – Airtel Broadband
submissions/ previews	2016-11-21T03:40:08Z	Kenya – Ebene, – Unknown African Network Information Center – Airtel Broadband
Submissions	2016-11-21T03:40:06Z	Kenya – Ebene, – Unknown African Network Information Center – Airtel Broadband
Assignments	2016-11-20T08:08:30Z	Kenya – Ebene, – Unknown African Network Information Center – APN IP Pool 2
submissions/ previews	2016-11-20T08:08:25Z	Kenya – Ebene, – Unknown African Network Information Center – APN IP Pool 2
Submissions	2016-11-20T08:08:22Z	Kenya – Ebene, – Unknown African Network Information Center – APN IP Pool 2
Assignments	2016-11-20T07:59:57Z	Kenya – Ebene, – Unknown African Network Information Center – APN IP Pool 2
submissions/ downloads	2016-11-17T09:36:29Z	United States – Los Angeles, – CA HugeServer Networks, LLC
submissions/ previews	2016-11-17T09:36:26Z	United States – Los Angeles, – CA HugeServer Networks, LLC
Submissions	2016-11-17T09:36:25Z	United States – Los Angeles, – CA HugeServer Networks, LLC
submissions/ previews	2016-11-17T09:27:12Z	United States – Los Angeles, – CA HugeServer Networks, LLC

(Continued)

Table B (Continued)

Lms Activity Code	Date/Time (Zulu)	Ip Address Translation
Submissions	2016-11-17T09:27:10Z	United States – Los Angeles, – CA HugeServer Networks, LLC
submissions/ downloads	2016-11-17T09:22:02Z	United States – Atlanta, – GA Cox Communications Inc. – Cox Communications
submissions/ previews	2016-11-17T09:21:46Z	United States – Los Angeles, – CA HugeServer Networks, LLC
Submissions	2016-11-17T09:21:38Z	United States – Atlanta, – GA Cox Communications Inc. – Cox Communications
submissions/ previews	2016-11-17T01:03:52Z	United States – Los Angeles, – CA HugeServer Networks, LLC
Submissions	2016-11-17T01:03:50Z	United States – Los Angeles, – CA HugeServer Networks, LLC
Assignments	2016-11-17T00:03:12Z	United States – Los Angeles, – CA HugeServer Networks, LLC
submissions/ previews	2016-11-17T00:03:06Z	United States – Los Angeles, – CA HugeServer Networks, LLC
Submissions	2016-11-17T00:03:04Z	United States – Los Angeles, – CA HugeServer Networks, LLC
submissions/ previews	2016-11-15T20:16:09Z	Kenya – Ebene, – Unknown African Network Information Center – APN IP Pool 2
Submissions	2016-11-15T20:16:07Z	Kenya – Ebene, – Unknown African Network Information Center – APN IP Pool 2
Assignments	2016-11-13T15:54:33Z	Kenya – Ebene, – Unknown African Network Information Center – Airtel Broadband
Assignments	2016-11-13T08:21:29Z	Kenya – Ebene, – Unknown African Network Information Center - Airtel Broadband
Assignments	2016-11-12T14:56:31Z	Kenya – Ebene, – Unknown African Network Information Center – APN IP Pool 2
Assignments	2016-11-12T14:55:48Z	Kenya – Ebene, – Unknown African Network Information Center – APN IP Pool 2
Assignments	2016-11-12T14:54:47Z	Kenya – Ebene, – Unknown African Network Information Center – APN IP Pool 2

Jane suspects: "I'm willing to bet that this student hired a surrogate to complete and submit their assignments for them."

Jane filed a student integrity incident report and presented the student and the academic review board with the evidence of unauthorized access and assignment completion.

Value Discussion

This case study primarily addresses the value of honesty. Students providing original work is crucial to the honesty and authenticity required of the learning process to ensure post-graduation and a future employer can expect mastery of the skills learned. University policy supports ethical standards for writing and assignment completion to ensure that the student who matriculates in their respective program is (a) the only one with access to their digital profile, (b) the only person responsible for attending in class (online and on ground), and (c) responsible for completion and submission of all assignments with original work and therefore grades directly represent authentic student performance.

Question Discussion

1. As a faculty member, what options does Jane have for ensuring authorized access to class by only students enrolled?
2. How does technology such as the use of virtual private networks (VPN's) or Tor-style browsers affect this scenario?
3. How does student surrogacy impact confidence by future employers in student skills mastery?
4. What role does the technical support (e.g., IT) play in addressing Jane's student honesty concerns?
5. What type of verification systems can remain flexible enough and allow an online student who is an airline pilot to submit papers from hotels, airports, mobile devices, etc. all in the same day yet generate a high degree of certainty that the submitter is actually the enrolled student?

Conclusion

The university must identify when learning and mastery of curriculum objectives is accomplished by someone other than the registered student. This requirement protects degree value, employment readiness, and school credibility.

Case 8: Foiling Attempts to Facilitate File Sharing: Updating Assessment

Ann M. Rogerson and Oriana Milani Price, University of Wollongong, Australia

Synopsis/Summary

Maressa, a faculty member at a large/mid-sized university in Australia must teach a large first year subject previously taught by someone else. Administrators have advised that assessment tasks had not been routinely updated, and students lacked model answer examples showing what was expected. Maressa has been tasked to address these issues. Hearing anecdotally that examples were not being provided as students were uploading them for credit on file sharing sites, she wants to address the issues but also limit students sharing her teaching materials and their completed assessments.

Supporting Information

Maressa recalled part of the meeting with the faculty administrators.

"We have received some student complaints about this subject and the assessments. One student was the third family member taking the course and had been tempted to use his brother's submission from two years ago as the assessment question asked had not changed and his brother received full marks. He queried why he should bother writing something new and queried the quality of our teaching."

Maressa had not realized the full impact of not changing assessment tasks, nor why providing model answer examples to students was a good idea until she had sat in on the last school meeting discussing the previous session of teaching.

Faculty member 1 said, "I learned about this type of thing the hard way, I wondered why there were so many text matches to other students within my class. Students referenced a site selling assignments where there were examples of work related to the theory in the question. When I spoke to the students about it, they said they did not understand how to present that type of response, so did a simple Google search and found the site. Obviously, many did the same thing hence the number of matches to the same material. They thought by referencing the site it was OK."

Faculty member 2 was very frustrated. "I heard from a colleague that it was a good idea to occasionally do an Internet search of the subject you were teaching. Wow. I was totally shocked. There were hits to one of those sites where students share things and there were my lecture notes plus the student had uploaded their assignment boasting that it got a high grade. They even left their name and student number!"

Value Discussion

This case study encourages individuals to be honest in their educational pursuits and acknowledge the original source of assessment materials. It also seeks to encourage a key underpinning element of honesty, which is to be truthful in how one's work is represented to others. When individuals represent the work of others as their own, they are being untruthful about their abilities to execute an assigned task. Being dishonest and untruthful undermines the potential for trust to develop.

Responsibility is the secondary value addressed in this case study. Every individual must do their part to promote academic integrity, while also taking steps to ensure that they take responsibility for their own work and ensuring that others are acknowledged for theirs. It also demonstrates good behavior which underpins responsibility. By sharing an example of what might have been done differently and sharing one's own mistakes, individuals can become role models for others by being accountable for one's own actions even when they may have been incorrect. This may provide a platform for developing a learning community of practice.

Question Discussion

1. How can faculty take responsibility for ensuring assessment tasks are refreshed and strengthened from session to session to support the honest completion of student work?
2. What can Maressa do to provide model answer examples to students while preventing the inappropriate sharing of her work?

3. Besides informing students that assessments are routinely updated and sample answers are also changed, what else can Maressa do to encourage students to take responsibility and ensure they honestly do their own work?

Conclusion

In order to promote honesty in assessment and foil attempts to share files and answers we need to take responsibility in educating our students about sound academic practice and the importance of honesty and responsibility in the work they submit for grading.

References

Bretag, T., Mahmud, S., Wallace, M., Walker, R., McGowan, U., East, J., Green, M., Partridge, L., and James, C. "Teach us how to do it properly!' An Australian academic integrity student survey," *Studies in Higher Education* 39, no. 7 (2014): 1150–1169, https://doi.org/10.1080/03075079.2013.777406.

Ellis, C., van Haeringen, K., Harper, R., Bretag, T., Zucker, I., McBride, S., Rozenberg, P., Newton, P., and Saddiqui, S. (2020). "Does authentic assessment assure academic integrity? Evidence from contract cheating data," *Higher Education Research & Development* 39, no. 3 (2020): 454–469.

Harper, R., Bretag, T., and Rundle, K. (2020). "Detecting contract cheating: Examining the role of assessment type," *Higher Education Research & Development* (2020): 1–16.

Lines, L. "Ghostwriters guaranteeing grades? The quality of online ghostwriting services available to tertiary students in Australia," *Teaching in Higher Education* 21, no. 8 (2016): 889–914. https://doi.org/10.1080/13562517.2016.1198759.

Rogerson, A. M. "Detecting contract cheating in essay and report submissions: Process, patterns, clues and conversations," *International Journal for Educational Integrity*, 13, no. 1 (2017). doi:10.1007/s40979-017-0021-6

Sheridan, L., and Rogerson, A. M. "Protecting our own copyright: Combating the piracy of academic content by students." Paper presented at the International Center for Academic Integrity (ICAI) Conference, Portland, OR, USA, 6–8 March, 2020.

Case 9: Caught in the Act

Tay McEdwards, Oregon State University, United States

Synopsis/Summary

P.J. is a testing assistant at an accredited university in the US. As part of his duties, he routinely assists faculty with concerns about online exams that require proctoring. While reviewing a video of an exam session proctored by a third-party online proctoring vendor, P.J. noticed that before the exam started the screen share captured an open Excel spreadsheet. This spreadsheet has thousands of entries about student information and appeared to be used for organized contract cheating.

Supporting Information

P.J. captured images of the spreadsheet which was used by the exam-taker to log into the LMS as a student and take the exam. The exam-taker used a photo ID that matched the name of the student and logged in to take the exam. After reviewing the spreadsheet in greater detail, it showed multiple tabs and columns listing thousands of entries for various institutions, student names, emails, ID numbers, and passwords. Next, P.J. reviewed exam sessions for multiple courses and students listed on the spreadsheet at his institution. It became clear that the same individual was posing as multiple students in various courses and taking exams. It was very likely that this individual was doing the same thing at other institutions listed on the spreadsheet.

Generally, P.J. delivers unusual findings directly to the instructor of a course so they can handle the situation as they deem appropriate. However, this type of situation including multiple student names, courses, instructors, and institutions had never been identified or captured on video recordings before. Due to this being a new type of situation, P.J. partnered with his supervisor and compiled all of the documentation that he could.

Value Discussion

The primary value in this case is honesty. Honesty forms the indispensable foundation of integrity and is a prerequisite for full realization of trust, fairness, respect, and responsibility. Examples of honesty in academia are to be truthful, give credit to the owner of work, provide factual information, and aspire to objectivity. Organized contract cheating for hire is a direct violation of honesty and truthfulness in academia. It is a form of cheating where an individual is hired to act as a student to complete the entire course and all of the work. This case study aligns with the fundamental value of honesty due to the lack of truthfulness, factual information, and credit to the owner involved with organized contract cheating. When an individual is hired to act as a student and complete all of their coursework, it can be difficult to prevent through traditional methods and requires an organized approach to identify factual information.

A secondary value for this case is responsibility. Responsibility identifies that upholding the values of integrity is simultaneously an individual duty and a shared concern. Examples of responsibility in academic life include engaging in difficult conversations, knowing, and following institutional rules and policies, holding yourself accountable for your actions, following through with tasks and expectations, and modeling good behavior. Contract cheating has occurred for decades, and this case study highlights one way in which it has evolved as an industry with online learning to continue to prosper from academia. Institutions have their own rules and policies with clear responsibilities and expectations. However, this situation showcases how institutional policies may not impact an industry that spans multiple institutions. This type of situation includes both an individual and shared concern to help us reflect on what responsibility and modeling good behavior could look like for institutions.

Question Discussion

1. Are there certain actions that P.J. and his supervisor should take next based on this situation?
2. What responsibility, if any, does the institution have to share information with the other institutions named on the organized contract cheating spreadsheet, and can they do so without violating governing education regulations?
3. What role does the student integrity office play when this type of organized cheating potentially impacts several institutions? The student code of conduct at most institutions clearly defines a policy and process for addressing students when involved in cheating. Does that apply to this type of organized cheating for hire?

4. What role does the administration play in addressing this type of organized contract cheating? What measures could be put in place by the institution's administration to reduce this type of organized cheating from occurring in the future?

Conclusion

Organized contract cheating undermines the foundation of honesty in academia and impacts many institutions by falling outside of their academic integrity policies and procedures, which focus on individual students.

Case 10: To Burn Bridges or to Build Them?

Blaire N. Wilson and Jason T. Ciejka, Emory University, United States

Synopsis/Summary

A staff member, Greg, proposes a solution to a staffing problem in the office during a team meeting. The solution is implemented successfully and praised by the senior leadership. Greg learned this idea from a colleague, Anna, who participates in a professional development group with him. After learning that he is receiving an award for this innovative solution, Greg considers whether he should share that this idea came from Anna.

Supporting Information

Greg was promoted to an assistant director two years ago and is considered by others to be a climber. He began working in the office three years earlier as a program coordinator. Greg just completed his master's degree and a professional development program for rising leaders at the institution. Greg has recently learned that his supervisor is leaving for a position at another institution and is interested in applying for this associate director position.

Anna has been an associate director for six years in a different department at the university. She has felt stuck in her position without a clear next opportunity. Anna has found collaborating with campus partners to be the most rewarding aspect of her position. Anna is completing the same professional development program for rising leaders as Greg. She hopes the completion of this program will aid in her pursuit of a promotion to director or in vying for another position on campus.

In an earlier meeting of their professional development program, Anna and Greg were partnered for an exercise. During the exercise, Greg vented to Anna about how their office was facing staffing issues and desperately seeking a creative solution. Anna shared with Greg an idea about creating graduate fellowships that would give graduate students professional experience while giving his office valuable staff time at the price of the graduate student stipend rather than a full staff salary.

Value Discussion

The primary value for this case is honesty. Taking credit for ideas that are not your own is in direct conflict with the value of honesty. Any community built on trust relies on honest actors within the community to establish a culture of integrity. A campus community includes staff members and administrators. They, too, should model the values of the community they support and serve. In this scenario, Greg has used Anna's idea and presented it as if it were his own. Greg is not displaying honest behavior.

Question Discussion

1. In what ways has Greg's actions created a disadvantage for Anna?
2. What assumptions did you make about Greg's motivations?
3. Imagine that Anna learns that Greg's office has implemented her idea. How should Anna respond in the situation? How would you approach addressing this conflict with Greg?
4. As a staff member, where do you draw the line when you are inspired by a colleague?
5. Imagine you are Greg's supervisor; how would you respond if he decided to be honest about where the idea originated?

Conclusion

Giving credit where credit is due is fundamental to a culture of honesty; institutions that encourage students, faculty, and staff to value integrity must create a consistent message that this is a priority.

Case 11: A Syllabus Sleight of Hand

Jason T. Ciejka and Blaire N. Wilson, Emory University, United States

Synopsis/Summary

A faculty member, Dr. Euclid, is designing a syllabus for a new course that will be reviewed by the university's curriculum committee. He has had low enrollments in previous courses and plans to request that this course meet the new quantitative reasoning graduation requirement to attract more students. The faculty adds several assignments to the proposed syllabus that will meet the standards of the new requirement, but he has no intention of following through on these once the course is approved.

Supporting Information

Dr. Euclid has taught in the social sciences at Decatur University for several years. His department chair has expressed concern that Dr. Euclid's course enrollments have been too low and has encouraged Dr. Euclid to consider different ways to drum up enrollment. The University recently approved a change to its graduation requirements replacing one course in mathematics with a course in quantitative reasoning. The course can be taught in any field as long as it incorporates quantitative approaches and at least 30 percent of the course grade is based on assignments that involve quantitative methods. Dr. Euclid believes that if his course carries the new quantitative reasoning designation, it will attract students who are reluctant to take more traditional mathematical and quantitative courses.

Dr. Euclid's research and courses are more qualitative in nature, but he surmises that once his course is approved for the new requirement, he can drop some of the quantitative material since the curriculum committee doesn't police existing courses. He shares this plan with the department chair as he prepares the proposal for the curriculum committee and asks the chair for the departmental letter of support that is required for the proposal.

Value Discussion

The primary value within this case is honesty. Dr. Euclid's plan to deceive the university curriculum committee represents a breach of the fundamental value of honesty. Although his proposed syllabus might meet the standards for approval on the surface, he has no intention of following his own syllabus when he teaches the course. If the department chair, knowing Dr. Euclid's plan, provides a letter of support for the proposal, this would represent a second act of dishonesty.

A secondary value within the case is responsibility. Dr. Euclid has a responsibility to follow the university's expectations in developing his course to meet the quantitative reasoning requirement. He is aware of the stipulations to offer such a course, and if his course is approved, he has the responsibility to follow through and offer the course in a way that is consistent with the requirement. His department chair has the additional responsibility of vetting the course before submitting a letter of support for the proposal. The system of proposing and approving courses depends on individuals holding themselves accountable to the university's standards.

Another secondary value within the case is courage. Dr. Euclid's decision to deceive the curriculum committee may reflect his fear of the decreasing enrollments in his class. He may also be reluctant to address the issue through more honest means that would require more attention. His department chair has the opportunity to act with courage by having a difficult conversation with Dr. Euclid about why furnishing a letter of support for the course would not be appropriate and by supporting Dr. Euclid to find other ways to revise his courses to increase their enrollment.

Question Discussion

1. What is the duty of faculty members to produce course materials in an honest and transparent way?
2. If the course is approved, how does this impact students, faculty, and the institution?
3. If you were a student in this course, and it was taught without the quantitative components, how would you respond?

Conclusion

Accreditation standards across universities rely heavily on the integrity of the institution, and the responsibility of individual faculty and programs to follow expectations.

Chapter 2
Trust

Chapter Contents:

Where in the Metaverse Is Boris' Voice
  Vivienne Blake, EF Academy, United States
  David Collett, Independent Consultant, Switzerland
  Alexa Mazarakis, International School Basel, Switzerland
Machine Learning: Trusting the Training Data, or the Trainer
  Michael S. Wills, Embry-Riddle Aeronautical University, United States
Clear as . . . Mud
  Sara Kellogg, Iowa State University, United States
Reduce, Reuse, Recycle
  Sara Kellogg, Iowa State University, United States
But They'll Never Know
  Blaire N. Wilson and Jason T. Ciejka, Emory University, United States
Suspicious Success
  Sara Kellogg, Iowa State University, United States
Capturing the Impostor Syndrome Through Turnitin
  Emilienne Idorenyin Akpan, American University of Nigeria, Nigeria
Pressure vs. Courage: The Dean's Dilemma
  Jason T. Ciejka and Blaire N. Wilson, Emory University, United States
My Students, My Research Subjects—Trust in Faculty, Researcher, and Student Relationships
  Tanja Fritz and Martin Daumiller, University of Augsburg, Germany
Using Relational Coordination to Promote Academic Integrity
  Matt Rahimian, Huron at Western University, Canada

Telling Family Secrets
   Claude E. P. Mayo, Quinnipiac University, United States
What Do You Mean Students Are in Charge?
   Jason T. Ciejka and Blaire N. Wilson, Emory University, United States

Trust is the ability to rely on the truth of someone or something. It is a fundamental pillar of academic pursuit. Within academics, we can promote trust by clearly stating our expectations and follow through on those expectations. That is whether we are faculty in the classroom and we are clearly stating the expectations for an assignment or if we are at the institution level where we are stating our expectations for academic integrity and what and how we will respond when breaches occur. Trust helps us promote transparency. Examples of trust in academia are to clearly state expectations, promote transparency, give credence, act with genuineness, and encourage mutual understanding. We want to trust others as we want to be trusted ourselves. We hold each other accountable to trust one another and encourage each other with a mutual understanding and act with genuineness when we have trust.

There are 12 case studies in this book which address the primary value of trust.

Case Studies Focused on the Student. There are five case studies which primarily address the student perspective.

Two of the cases deal with the ever-expanding role of predictive text and artificial intelligence. In "Case 1: *Where in the Metaverse Is Boris' Voice*" a student struggles with developing his writing skills when his computer completes sentences for him resulting in the teacher and librarian questioning the authenticity of the assignment. In "Case 2: *Machine Learning: Trusting the Training Data, or the Trainer*" a student uses some vendor-provided machine learning models but struggles to understand the models and data and inappropriately uses the vendor data.

The remaining three case studies address various forms of reuse and collaboration. In "Case 3: *Clear as . . . Mud*" students are permitted to work together in a chemistry lab, though required to submit individual reports. When the reports look remarkably similar, the teacher questions the collaboration. In "Case 4: *Reduce, Reuse, Recycle*" a student is retaking a course failed in a previous semester and the student turns in a paper from the previous course while the course requirement is to submit original work. The student believes the work is original to him and should be graded without penalty. In "Case 5: *But They'll Never Know*" a student working on a group project stumbles upon an answer key that includes the exact problem the professor assigned to their group. The student presents this as one of her solutions without disclosing where she found the solution.

Case Studies Focused on the Faculty and/or Administrator. There are four case studies which primarily address this perspective.

In "Case 6: *Suspicious Success*" an instructor receives a request from a student who missed many classes and nearly fails an extension for a major assignment. The instructor denies the request, but when the assignment is submitted on time and receives high marks, the instructor is convinced the work was completed dishonestly.

In "Case 7: *Capturing the Impostor Syndrome Through Turnitin*" Turnitin is used to encourage students to work better with their instructors, use the writing center more, and trust in their critical reading, thinking, note-making, writing, and referencing abilities.

In "Case 8: *Pressure vs. Courage: The Dean's Dilemma*" the dean is being pressured by the president of the university about an academic misconduct case involving the daughter of a public official. The integrity board has recommended that the student receive a failing grade in the course, but the president suggests a lighter sanction, such as a verbal warning.

In "*Case 9: My Students, My Research Subjects—Trust in Faculty, Researcher, and Student Relationships*" a faculty member surveyed students in multiple courses at his university to assess the extent of cheating behavior. Lower cheating rates in his own courses compared to his colleagues' make him question whether his students' feared repercussions on their grades in his courses if they answered truthfully.

Case Studies Focused on the Academic Integrity Office. The remaining three case studies primarily address this perspective.

In "Case 10: *Using Relational Coordination to Promote Academic Integrity*" an academic integrity officer faces issues on how to convince various stakeholders to invest in academic integrity initiatives and go beyond a standard policy.

In "Case 11: *Telling Family Secrets*" a student claims that a faculty member shared information about an integrity case with her stepson.

The student posits that the confidentiality breach has compromised the adjudication process, his reputation, and FERPA.

In "Case 12: *What Do You Mean Students Are in Charge?*" the president of the University Senate has asked the Senate to consider making changes to the student-governed honor system. She was disappointed that a student she reported for academic misconduct was not found responsible by the student honor council and believes that faculty must be on the hearing boards with voting power.

In addition to the twelve case studies in this chapter on trust, four other case studies in this book address trust as a secondary value. Refer to that value chapter as shown for an introduction to each case study.

Honesty:

- *Photoshop: The Easiest (Worst!) Way Out*

  Respect:

- *Personalized and Supportive Proctoring Processes*
- *When the Bones Are Good: Laying the Foundation for the Faculty*

  Responsibility:

- *That's Not Fair: Balancing the Workload for Remote Teams*

Case 1: Where in the Metaverse Is Boris' Voice

Vivienne Blake, EF Academy, United States; David Collett, Independent Consultant, Switzerland; Alexa Mazarakis, International School Basel, Switzerland

Synopsis/Summary

The teacher's comment, "I need to be able to trust you wrote this," was scrawled in digital ink on Boris' essay. He sighed. "But how? My computer auto completes sentences for me before I even know what I'm trying to say!" Boris wants to develop his writing skills, and his teacher and the librarian were teaching paraphrasing and citation without artificial intelligence (AI) tools. "But it's really hard to put things in your own words," he thought, "and what about my grade!?"

Supporting Information

As anyone who has written a Gmail lately can attest, artificial intelligence has improved to the degree where it is now possible to generate authentic computer written text without running afoul of plagiarism checkers. The way AI does this is complex but similar to how the human mind thinks—by making connections between variables and extrapolating from them using logic. Examples of the kinds of tools that students already have access to range in complexity, from highly sophisticated Hyperwrite.ai (https://hyperwrite.ai/) that can generate whole papers complete with citations, to something as simple as wordtune (https://www.wordtune.com/) that will rewrite paragraphs of text on the fly.

No matter how you look at it, this represents a new dimension to education. It used to be that "copying" from someone meant there was a clear "source" and method of detection/deterrent (i.e., plagiarism-checker like Turnitin.com). Now, however, "inauthentic" work is becoming increasingly undetectable. In a world where we can no longer verify authenticity in the same ways, we have to ensure that the values that we espouse—trust, respect and honesty—are truly at the heart of the learning process. There is no tech tool to fix this scenario. Thus, only when our values are embedded in the learning, and thus shortcuts are understood as cheating oneself out of the learning, will we be able to sustainably take advantage of these new tools, and not be taken advantage of by them.

Value Discussion

The primary value in this case is trust. In the metaverse, a new environment, individuals can be whomever they wish to be, and others may not know the real person behind the online identity. So, how can we count on everyone to be trustworthy? Realistically, we need to set clear expectations for an "ethical environment" where transactions, knowledge transfers, and educational tools promote transparency. This environment is based on the trustworthiness that student work, research, artwork, music, or other material, is produced honestly and accurately with clear citations crediting the work of others. Programming artificial intelligence tools requires an ethical approach that ensures trust is ever-present and reinforced.

A secondary value for this case is respect. All participants in the metaverse must understand that their online words and actions have real-world consequences. Thus, we must convey respect for others, whether they are known to us or not. We must also show respect to ourselves by maintaining a consistency between on- and off-line actions. Tools and institutions that comprise the metaverse must be designed with long-standing social values of respect and honesty.

Another secondary value is honesty, namely, to be truthful, all research and learning must be free from plagiarism, deception, or any kind of fraud. The integrity of our collective knowledge requires honesty to advance. Research and learning are a difficult process that must rely on our critical thinking and not merely on tools. Honesty supports the functioning of our human society, and thus the virtual extension of it, the metaverse.

Question Discussion

1. How do we enhance trust by ensuring we support and advocate for respecting the honest voice of the author?
2. How does a student learn to cite correctly so as to show where his/her voice starts/ends vs. the quoted information from an information source?
3. How do we vet sources of information and tools to ensure that what we acquire promotes these goals (i.e., we wouldn't subscribe to Cliff Notes)?
4. How do you find the source of voice for students in any assignment and protect your own voice? (rewording, and stealing)
5. How do we make assistive technology truly "assistive" and not a crutch?
6. How do we change our approach to education to make trust, respect, and honesty the goal, not just a "better method?"

Conclusion

Students need our help to develop and keep their own voice! Faculty and other resources need the way through the metaverse using trust, honesty, and respect to safeguard accuracy and originality.

Case 2: Machine Learning: Trusting the Training Data, or the Trainer

Michael S. Wills, Embry-Riddle Aeronautical University, United States

> Note: This case study does not require more than just conversational awareness that machine learning or applied artificial intelligence tools are in widespread use today; the same is true regarding students' and teachers' awareness of the laws and practices of countering financial crime and preventing money laundering. As such, this case study may also help demystify these technologies by its focus on the ethical issues involved, as it relates cutting-edge practice in business and industry to academic integrity issues.

Synopsis/Summary

Emil is a graduate student member of a team in Professor Wanda's class. His team is applying machine learning techniques to banking data, as part of an in-class role-playing business simulation, focusing on detecting fraud and other financial crimes. This simulation is part of Professor Wanda's grant-funded research activities. Emil is one of five students on Pieter's student team, which is using some vendor-provided machine learning models. Emil's first task is to train these models using a representative subset of their full data sets. Emil does not understand these models or the data and could not get them to work with the team's data. Instead, he has used demonstration data from the vendor, which seems to work, so he's told the team the models are ready to use.

Supporting Information

This case centers on the misrepresentation of data, and the impacts it may have on a team that relies that data. In this hypothetical situation, Professor Wanda has perhaps over-sold her student's capabilities to apply unfamiliar technologies and modeling techniques. She has placed the responsibility for this project on Emil, who has a general business student background; he is not a programmer/analyst, and does not have deep technical understanding of how the new system should work.

But rather than take the more difficult journey of learning how to use the system, he cheats. He moves a copy of the demonstration system, already trained on its vendor-supplied data, into the shared area for the rest of the team to start using, he covers this up, and allows Professor Wanda and his teammates to assume that the new system is now correctly trained and ready for work.

Pieter comes into the student lounge and finds Emil sitting and having a coffee, gazing out the window. "Hey Emil," he said, "I'm glad that you were finally able to get the new machine learning model set up and working well with the training data Professor Wanda provided us. It's running wonderfully—it's really helping the team speed up our analysis of possible fraud and money laundering cases. If that keeps up, we'll be able to get our overall findings together and brief Professor Wanda about our results on schedule. Thank you!"

"You're welcome, Pieter," said Emil, barely even turning to face Pieter. "Glad it's helping you out. I hope the others are happy too."

"I've heard that getting those machine learning systems trained up, and keeping them trained, takes a lot of data science," said Pieter. "I'd love to learn more about that system and how we're keeping it trained on what the bank is seeing in its own data," he added, hoping to get invited to see it in action. But Emil seemed hesitant. "I'm still learning to handle it properly," Emil said. "It's pretty complicated." He got up, said goodbye, and took his coffee and left.

Pieter was puzzled by Emil's demeanor. He seemed standoffish. He knew that the professor was really counting on their team to have meaningful results with this machine learning approach. She had used grant funding to get the software they were using, and access to the live, real-world data feeds that all of her student teams were analyzing. She was very concerned about the early delays that Pieter's team suffered in getting the models trained well enough to start using them for live analytical work.

Was Emil just stressed out? Or was there something bothering him? Pieter couldn't tell.

Value Discussion

The trustworthiness of any system (of any kind or technology) starts when its users and stakeholders share a common set of expectations about its objectives and processes. Those expectations become the standards of measurement that rely on transparency in that system. Falsifying the source of data used in any system jeopardizes the trustworthiness of that system's outcomes (as in the "fruit from the tainted tree" doctrine in law).

Honesty values data that is truthful; the use of honest data in logically transparent, understandable, and testable ways produces assertions or conclusions that are also honest. In systems terms, this attribute is called systems integrity: a system demonstrates integrity when it performs its required functions, and no others, in an unimpaired manner, and that is free from interference, manipulation, or undue influence by or from any unauthorized source.

The builders of a system have a duty of care (a responsibility) to those who will use it; those users have a shared concern as to whether that system works properly or not. They are relying upon the builder(s) for an honest, faithful report on the system's reliability, integrity, and accuracy when it is turned over to them for use. Without this, users have no idea of the risks they may be taking in counting on that system to meet their needs.

Question Discussion

The characters in this scenario have all made decisions based on their understanding of the ideas, concepts, and data that they or others have shared with them. It's also quite likely that each of them has made various assumptions, even subconsciously, regarding the team's activities. This can mean that the team members are working at cross purposes, all the while believing that they have a strong, collaborative working relationship in place. Arguably, the more tacit, unstated, and untested those assumptions, the more any team is relying upon blind trust, rather than informed consent and agreement.

Exploring This Case with the Question Formulation Technique. In starting to ask himself questions, Pieter is beginning to apply the Question Formulation Technique to this situation; he's on the journey of discovering if there is indeed something going on that is worth worrying about, as a prelude to thinking about taking any actions or voicing his concerns to anyone. In doing so, Pieter is enabling his natural curiosity to suggest various ideas to explore, triggered in part by the information that might (or might not) be evidence of a cause-and-effect relationship worth further investigation. You can pivot your use of the guiding questions by challenging students to respond in brainstorming fashion with their own questions that are triggered by the case, or by simple prompts you can draw from the guiding questions. Advise students to hold off on judging or attempting to respond to questions at first; instead, use the QFT to guide them in adding to or refining their sets of questions, and then letting their own intuitions focus them on those questions of theirs that attract their attention the most.

1. How do you determine whether a particular decision should rely on authority, analytical insight, or creative vision?
2. How can the characters in this case study separate personal agendas, interests, and needs from those of the context in which they exercise influence or responsibility by their actions?
3. Complex situations sometimes involve establishing compromises across differing agendas and stakeholder interests. How does the way in which you use, rely, or refer to the sources that inform your actions relate to your ability to honestly broker such compromises?
4. What practical or ethical considerations could have been applied to prevent or preclude actions that put the team in this situation? Which character or characters seem to have been best positioned to make such judgment calls?
5. People need to be able to place their trust and confidence in the decision processes that impact their lives, work, or interests; in trusting such decision processes, people must also tacitly or explicitly trust how secure those processes are. Decision assurance therefore requires a degree of information security, that is, taking steps to protect the confidentiality, integrity, availability, non-reputability, authenticity, privacy, and safety aspects of the information used by a system and the actions taken based on that information. How might an information security-based perspective on decision assurance be applied to this scenario?
6. Across every industry, organizations are adopting similar machine learning models and adapting their decision-making processes to

gain or maintain the advantages they desire in their marketplaces, contexts, or cultures. Is this a decision that should be left to the individual organization, or do societies need to take a more active role here?

Conclusion

Trust is not just a classroom concept; this case shows its necessity as organizations rely on their people using trustworthy processes and systems to make decisions and produce real value.

Case 3: Clear as . . . Mud

Sara Kellogg, Iowa State University, United States

Synopsis/Summary

Jason and Lee are classmates at an American accredited university. They are permitted to work together in a chemistry lab, though required to submit individual reports. While grading, their faculty determines their reports to be copied, so gives them a zero and refers the case to Student Conduct. The students believe that working together in the lab resulted in the similarities in their work and should not be considered misconduct.

Supporting Information

Jason and Lee are lab partners in chemistry. Their professor, Dr. Hanes, encourages students to work in pairs to conduct their lab experiments. To get credit and demonstrate their understanding, students are required to submit individual reports describing the lab activity and results. While grading their most recent reports, Dr. Hanes finds significant similarities in report organization and content that suggests Jason or Lee's report was copied by the other student with only minor differences. Dr. Hanes sends both students emails stating, "Your individual lab reports appear nearly identical, suggesting academic misconduct. I cannot give you credit for the lab and will be referring this to Student Conduct."

Jason immediately contacts the student conduct office to schedule meetings, sharing his surprise at the allegation. During their meetings, both students point to the syllabus, which states students can work together on the lab. Jason shares the reason the reports are so similar is because they did the work together and discussed the outcomes. Lee shares that Jason will typically set up and conduct the lab experiments while Lee documents the processes and reactions. Lee notes, "Afterwards, we always discuss our findings and then write our reports." Both students deny copying and claim they completed their reports independently as required.

Value Discussion

The primary value explored in this case is trust. Students must ensure they are completing work within the guidelines provided by faculty, consult about any lack of clarity, and trust that if their work is completed honestly that this should be evident. Faculty, without evidence to the contrary, may need to trust that students had no intent to engage in misconduct.

A secondary value in this case is fairness. Students may need to acknowledge where their work was too similar, or their collaboration exceeded faculty's expectations, and understand that faculty must review work under consistent guidelines as indicated for assessing all students in the course. Faculty may need to review and revise guidance in the syllabus or on specific coursework addressing their expectations for student collaboration.

Question Discussion

1. Where faculty permit collaboration on coursework, what expectations should they have for students submitting individual work?
2. How might students approach collaboration in a manner that allows them to still submit independent work pertaining to a project?
3. What level of responsibility should be assigned to the students where instructions or guidelines are found to be ambiguous?

Conclusion

In every conflict there are opportunities for both sides to consider how they could have avoided the issue, and willingness to do so can result in improved engagement and trust.

Case 4: Reduce, Reuse, Recycle

Sara Kellogg, Iowa State University, United States

Synopsis/Summary

Joe is a student at an American accredited university and is retaking a course which he failed in a previous semester. Joe's faculty reports him for plagiarism and assigns a zero on his paper as Turnitin identified it as nearly identical to a paper he'd submitted last semester for the same course, and there is a course requirement for work submitted to be original. Joe believes his work is original to him and should be graded without penalty.

Supporting Information

Joe is retaking Philosophy 277 because he received a failing grade last semester. He believes he's retained much of what he learned in his previous attempt at the course and is optimistic his grade will improve. Joe submits his midterm paper feeling confident about the work. Dr. Alvarez finds that Joe's paper is flagged for plagiarism by Turnitin. During the next class, Dr. Alvarez asks Joe to stay after to discuss.

During their meeting, Dr. Alvarez asks Joe to explain how he went about writing his paper, expressing his concerns. Joe responds, "I took the course previously and had a lot of resources on this topic that I was able to use to write my paper." Dr. Alvarez indicates this is a problem and shows Joe the syllabus where it states all work for the course must be original. He also shows Joe the Turnitin report that identifies his self-plagiarism. He tells Joe that he plans to give him a zero and has to report him for academic misconduct.

Joe disagrees with this outcome, sharing he did all the research and writing for the paper. He states that he submitted his own work for the same requirement in the same course. Joe also notes that he made modifications and improvements to this semester's paper based on additional research. Joe argues he should not be penalized or reported and should receive the grade earned for his paper.

Value Discussion

The primary value in this case is trust. To protect the confidence faculty have in the integrity of a student's work, students may benefit from proactively addressing academic behavior or decision-making that might deviate from faculty's expectations or stated course goals.

A secondary value found in this case is fairness. Students expect faculty to fairly assess completed work and believe they should not be penalized for what they may perceive as technicalities or misunderstandings. Faculty must fairly enforce course policies, including those times when a student violates a policy they may not have fully understood. Faculty may also need to consider how and when discretion is best applied.

Question Discussion

1. What would be the appropriate interpretation of "original work" (the student's or faculty's) to apply in this case?
2. Is the faculty in this case being unreasonable?
3. What potential learning outcomes for this assignment are lost with the student submitting their repurposed paper?
4. What other strategies might faculty use to address this situation other than failure and referral?

Conclusion

Rules and guidelines are important to clarify expectations, but some situations may present more compelling cases for consideration in trust of the student and flexibility in finding the best resolution.

Case 5: But They'll Never Know

Blaire N. Wilson and Jason T. Ciejka, Emory University, United States

Synopsis/Summary

Three students are assigned to a group project. The students agree to bring three solutions for the project to a brainstorming session. While researching, Leeann stumbles upon an answer key from a workbook that includes the exact problem the professor assigned to their group. Leeann presents this as one of her solutions at the brainstorming session without disclosing where she found the solution. Leeann changes some details to deviate from the answer key, and the group chooses to use Leeann's solution.

Supporting Information

Leeann is working in a group with Kellie and Taylor. Leeann knows Kellie from a student organization they have in common, while Leann and Taylor have other classes together in their political science major.

Leeann has been actively involved in the leadership of her student organization. She spends a lot of time on this work, but also works part-time at a coffee shop off campus about 10–15 hours each week.

Leeann has been overwhelmed by her job and her leadership position. She has always struggled with being organized, but in the past has been able to complete all of her tasks on time. It wasn't until recently that she noticed she is barely getting by.

Leeann had three weeks to research and plan solutions for the project, but she waited until the final week to begin researching.

The course is an introduction to city planning and their specific case study involves making budget cuts in a small city: Littletown. Littletown needs to make a 10 percent cut across their budget. The case study has clear criteria limiting certain cuts, which makes the problem tricky. Students are expected to explore the pros and cons of their proposed solution from various angles: public relations, political interests of Littletown, upcoming elections, and employee retention and compensation. While there isn't one correct answer, the professor notes that there is a "most informed/well advised" answer.

Value Discussion

Trust is the primary value within this case. Transparency is an important component of trust. In this scenario, Leeann is not being transparent with her group mates about her source. In a group setting, members must trust and rely on each other to achieve a state of genuine teamwork and for the project to succeed. When groups form, either organically or by assignment, is it reasonable for an individual to question the authenticity of their other groupmates' work? Trust in a community is built upon respect towards one another.

Honesty is a clear secondary value explored in this scenario. Leeann is dishonest by intentionally deciding not to disclose that she discovered the answer key for the scenario. This action breaches the expectation of trust within the group setting.

Respect, another secondary value, for others includes recognizing the consequences of your actions and how they impact others. Leeann is faced with a conflict that threatens to harm her reputation with her group. On the one hand, she risks disapproval from her group for not fully preparing her research. On the other hand, she risks jeopardizing her group through the possibility that the professor may discover her misconduct.

Question Discussion

1. How might Leeann's actions impact her own personal and professional goals?
2. How might Leeann's actions impact her peers?
3. How might Leeann's actions impact her instructor?
4. What could Leeann have done differently to avoid this situation?

Conclusion

Group work is based on trusting other collaborators to be an active part contributing to the end product. It also requires trust that each member is completing his/her part successfully in an honest manner.

Case 6: Suspicious Success

Sara Kellogg, Iowa State University, United States

Synopsis/Summary

Joanna is an instructor at an American accredited university and receives an email from a student who missed many classes and is nearly failing. The student requests an extension for a major assignment citing a personal emergency. Joanna does not believe any additional exceptions can be made, and shares if the assignment is late, it will not receive a grade. When it is submitted on time and receives high marks, Joanna is convinced the work was completed dishonestly.

Supporting Information

Joanna receives an email from Laila, a student enrolled in her Human Development course. Joanna recognizes Laila as a student who has missed class regularly, submitted late or sub-par assignments, and is at risk of failing the course. Laila's email states, "I had to leave school and go home because my mom is in the hospital, so I won't be in class this week. Could I please get an extension for my midterm project as I hardly leave the hospital right now, and I know I can't pass the class without a good grade on this assignment." Laila adds that she has documentation she could provide to support her request.

Joanna considers that she has already granted Laila three excused absences, which is the limit for her course absence policy. She responds to Laila, denying her extension request, and noting that she has had many weeks to complete the project. Joanna shares with Laila that if her project is not on time, she will get a zero. A few days later, on the due date, Joanna receives Laila's project submission. When grading, Joanna discovers the project to be high quality work, which is not reflective of Laila's overall performance in the class. Joanna is suspicious of Laila's submission, and convinced she must have completed the work dishonestly, so reaches out to the student conduct office to consult.

Value Discussion

The primary value in this case is trust. Faculty may have a basis for suspicion or doubt regarding academic integrity, but without evidence to the contrary, they may have to trust a student's word and work, even where previous experience has made this challenging. Students must understand the reciprocal nature of trust and recognize how their behavior and investment may make it difficult for faculty to believe them and/ or be willing to make exceptions.

Several secondary values can be seen in this case: honesty, responsibility, and fairness. Faculty have a responsibility to implement course expectations fairly and may be unable to use discretion where a student has repeatedly tested boundaries, even where circumstances may seem to support further consideration. Students must be honest with themselves and faculty about performance issues and course engagement and demonstrate regard for course policies. Students have a responsibility to complete coursework with integrity and should expect to be assessed appropriately for their effort.

Question Discussion

1. Is it appropriate for faculty to consider an additional exception for this request based upon the personal circumstances described?
2. Should the student's prior performance or engagement in the course be viewed as a contributing factor for suspected misconduct in this situation?
3. How should faculty respond where there is a strong suspicion of academic misconduct, but not necessarily clear evidence?
4. What is the best way for Joanna to engage with Laila going forward in the course?

Conclusion

Personal feelings regarding a student's engagement in a course, however well-founded, can influence trust and the ability to offer objective evaluation, even where suspicions are unsupported.

Case 7: Capturing the Impostor Syndrome Through Turnitin

Emilienne Idorenyin Akpan, American University of Nigeria, Nigeria

Synopsis/Summary

Ewi teaches freshman composition in a liberal arts college. He also works in the institution's writing center which organizes academic integrity workshops each semester. Prior to the school's subscription to Turnitin, some students doubted they were good enough while others avoided detection of academic integrity infractions. With Turnitin, instructors now have verifiable tools to identify misconduct, enhance the importance of academic resources available to the students, and emphasize sanctions for academic dishonesty. These measures have encouraged students to work better with their instructors, use the writing center more, and trust in their critical reading, thinking, note-making, writing, and referencing abilities.

Supporting Information

The transition from high school to college is an exciting milestone. However, issues—such as being away from home for the first time, setting unrealistic goals, understanding the academic expectations in higher education, and learning to work with new peers—may influence a student's confidence in their ability to fit in, learn, and perform as well.

"Have you uploaded your assignment yet?" asked Nado.

Rana looked up wearily at Nado. "I excelled in high school, but I always seem to be catching up here, as everyone else seems to be better." She squinted, then furtively copied, and pasted the remaining information.

"What are you doing this time? Didn't that article rewriter teach you anything?" Nado's eyes and mouth widened.

"There's no similarity against my work. There, I've finished." Rana uploaded the document before Canvas closed, snapped the laptop shut, and wriggled out of the chair.

"Remember the honor code," Nado warned. "And the integrity presentation."

"Academic writing is hard, and my work doesn't seem as good as the ones we read in class. I need As," Rana explained. "Why do we even have to write in all our courses?"

Another sigh. "This is our first semester, Rana, and we are all still learning! You don't join the study skills tutorials hosted by the writing center and Mr. Ewi has stressed why all assignments are now linked to Turnitin. Whoever is teaching these 'strategies' is not helping you. I don't need this trouble."

"My work has no errors." Rana smirked.

"That's not how to use Turnitin," Nado said.

The following week, Ewi completed the academic infraction form and clicked Send. "Rana, this time, you will receive a formal invitation to appear before the Academic Integrity Council."

"I'm sorry Mr. Ewi." Rana stooped over the printed Turnitin report, signed the charge sheet, and left.

Value Discussion

Trust is the primary value addressed in this case study. It is key in academic integrity because having confidence in a stakeholder's ability to do what is right keeps relationships open, respectful, and valuable. Self-trust is equally important to resist platforms or practices that promote unethical behavior and erode confidence in one's competencies. Rana did not trust her abilities to produce acceptable work or to build the necessary competencies required for college writing tasks. She also did not avail herself of the resources which support the learning process. These made her susceptible to wrong choices as her only focus became obtaining great letter grades by any means.

Honesty, as the secondary value addressed in this case study, begins with oneself, and it builds character. It should be nurtured and protected especially in the midst of tempting unethical practices. Dishonesty leads to doubts, estrangement, and sanctions. It also affects credibility, taints the student's academic records, and can bring the institution into disrepute. Without honesty, it is difficult to trust or respect a person no matter how close or respectable they may seem.

Respect is also a value addressed in this case study. It is two-ways, and it is also earned. It promotes self-interrogation, active listening, effective learning, openness to ideas, awareness of what is unacceptable, and resistance to what will invariably cause disappointment, hurt, and shame. Respect demonstrates esteem of self and the other, and where unacceptable conduct is intentional, there is no regard for engagements with either persons or the institution that values transparency, hard work, and honesty.

Responsibility is the final secondary value addressed in this case study. It is about being accountable for one's actions or inactions. The intentional violation of clearly defined policies that promote academic integrity should be penalized—as stated in the relevant codes—by the authorized parties to deter further dishonest behaviors. Responsibility also means taking the right action without bias when infractions have been identified or being brave enough to resist unnecessary pressures which can lead to poor decision-making instances and regrettable outcomes.

Question Discussion

1. What factors make different forms of academic dishonesty attractive to new college students?
2. Are there valid concerns which challenge trusting the functionality of Turnitin in academia?
3. How can writing centers work effectively with faculty and students to encourage honest scholarship?
4. To what extent should academic integrity only apply to institutions with (digital) resources that facilitate learning, personal development, and best practices?

Conclusion

With guidance, students can use Turnitin properly to understand nuances in language, progressively master the principles of academic writing, familiarize themselves with the formats of referencing styles, enhance awareness of the values of academic integrity, and believe in their abilities to produce trustworthy work that they can confidently defend.

Case 8: Pressure vs. Courage: The Dean's Dilemma

Jason T. Ciejka and Blaire N. Wilson, Emory University, United States

Synopsis/Summary

Dean Li has received a call from the president of the college, President Henderson, about an academic misconduct case involving Leila, the daughter of a public official. The integrity board has recommended that the student receive a failing grade in the course. President Henderson has asked Dean Li to consider a lighter sanction like a verbal warning when she issues the final decision.

Supporting Information

Dean Li is the academic dean of a small college and reports directly to President Henderson. Dean Li assumed the role of dean this year after President Henderson encouraged her to apply for the position. As part of her many responsibilities, Dean Li makes all final decisions in academic misconduct cases according to the college's academic integrity policy. Dean Li receives a recommendation from the academic integrity board but is free to make her own decisions in cases. Dean Li is aware that her predecessors almost always accepted the recommendation of the academic integrity board and only deviated in rare circumstances when the recommendation did not accord with precedent.

Dean Li is currently reviewing the decision of the academic integrity board to find Leila, a junior at the college, responsible for cheating on a midterm exam. Leila was apparently aware that another student had to take the exam early, and she paid her to take photos of the test to share with her. Leila denied the allegations, but the evidence was overwhelming and the academic integrity board recommended failure of the course.

President Henderson has called Dean Li to ask if there is any leeway for the sanction in this case. Leila is the daughter of a public official, and although the college is private, it has a close relationship with the official and depends on a number of state and local grants and collaborations. Dean Li informs the president that the case is quite serious, but President Henderson suggests that she issue the lightest possible sanction—a verbal warning.

Value Discussion

The primary value in this case is trust. Academic leaders require a level of trust to operate both effectively and ethically in their positions. Trust requires transparency in decision-making, open lines of communication, and shared values around integrity. In this case, the level of trust appears to be eroded by the pressure to allow external factors to influence the academic integrity process. There is still an opportunity to restore trust by engaging in an honest dialogue that reaffirms the values of the institution and the importance of upholding the academic integrity process.

A secondary value for this case is fairness. Students should receive impartial treatment in an academic integrity process no matter who they are or what connections they have through family or other means. Treating a student differently because of factors like an influential parent undermines the commitment to fairness in this system. Although academic integrity processes are private and confidential, rumors have a way of spreading in colleges and universities. If other students had the sense that a student was treated differently because of her family connections, this could greatly damage the perceived fairness of the system.

Another secondary value in this case is courage. Academic integrity requires the exercise of courage. Individuals should strive to do what's right even when there is pressure to act differently. In this case, the dean may have some fear of disappointing the president or making the work of the college more difficult by upsetting the local official. As a leader at the institution, the dean also has an obligation to defend the academic integrity process and to inform the president of the consequences of changing the decision, such as weakening the faith of students and faculty in the system and the leadership of the institution.

Question Discussion

1. How do administrators tactfully respond when they face pressures that may be inappropriate or ethically suspect?
2. When should an administrator trust their own judgment over the judgment of integrity boards and the strength of the process?
3. In what ways would a decision to change a student's recommended sanctions based on their family connections undermine academic integrity at an institution?

Conclusion

Administrators who oversee academic integrity often face pressure from other colleagues and offices to intervene in individual cases, which carries the risk of undermining the policy and culture of integrity.

Case 9: My Students, My Research Subjects—Trust in Faculty, Researcher, and Student

Tanja Fritz and Martin Daumiller, University of Augsburg, Germany

Synopsis/Summary

Ron, a faculty member and researcher on academic dishonesty, surveyed students in multiple courses at his university to assess the extent of cheating behavior in exams and other assignments. Lower cheating rates in his own courses compared to his colleagues' make him question whether his students' feared repercussions on their grades in his courses if they answered truthfully.

Supporting Information

To make sense of the survey results, Ron decides to engage his students in a discussion about his worries. Upon asking whether some of them might have been hesitant to participate in the survey in fear of repercussions, again ensuring his neutrality, one student responds: "I have taken several courses you teach, and I had noted that you always admitted to errors or when you didn't know something. That identifies a sincere person to me, so I trusted that you wouldn't utilize this survey against us."

In the further discussion, Ron approaches his students as experts in their own right on the topic of academic dishonesty and encourages them to share their insights into reasons for cheating on assessments. He learns that students acknowledge if a lecturer really cares about them learning, which in turn motivates them to engage with the material. As a counterexample, one student shares her sentiment: "In one course we quickly learned that the lecturer didn't really read the essays we had to give in. We never received any feedback on our writing either. Some of us then started to just copy stuff from the internet as the lecturer didn't seem to care, as long as we submitted something. For me, it really reduced the effort I was willing to put into it, with all the other semester assignments due." Ron commits to taking what he has learned through the discussion to the next faculty meeting. Together with the students he explores the possibility of involving a student council to debate integrity at the university on both the student and faculty side.

Value Discussion

Trust is the primary value in this case. The portraited case exemplifies how trust in teacher-student relationships can be established by genuine communication. Being honest about one's own fallibilities while teaching shows sincerity and fosters a safe atmosphere for students to show equal honesty. When Ron the teacher assumed a simultaneous role as a researcher of his students' dishonest behavior, he made sure to communicate his intentions with his research transparently and assured that students won't be affected by the answers they provide. As he showed an adherence to such agreements, he had encouraged his students to an open discussion based on mutual understanding.

Honesty, respect, responsibility, and courage are all secondary values within this case. With respect to honesty, the case also illustrates how academic dishonesty can be effectively approached from a neutral stance. Objectivity and an interest in understanding improvable causes of student cheating behavior can facilitate a mutual investigation between teachers and students. Before inviting his students to participate in his survey on the issue, Ron made sure to approach the discussion from a factual and honest standpoint as a researcher, as well as when communicating the survey results and his worries about a potential reluctance to disclose dishonest behavior in his own lectures.

Respect can be seen when an eye level approach in teacher-student relationships acknowledges students as active participants in the educational experience. Exemplifying such a respectful approach in the scenario, Ron sparked an open discussion about academic dishonesty with his students by emphasizing their unique insights into reasons why cheating occurs. By inviting them to take their experiences to a debate together with other faculty members, he encouraged students to give feedback and to participate as co-creators in the learning environment.

With respect to responsibility, Ron sees his responsibility as a teacher and researcher to not shy away from difficult discussions—with his students as well as his colleagues. He wants to credit the students' perspective by taking action to improve institutional practices, thereby acting as a role model for the behavior he wants to encourage in his students. By inviting them to play an active part in that discussion, he also gives them the opportunity to take up responsibilities as equal members of the academic environment.

Courage is the final value seen in this case. Among Ron's faculty colleagues, there might be some holding the belief that "some students are just lazy" and that "a certain amount of cheating is to be expected." For Ron to confront his colleagues about the fallacy behind such beliefs and their own potential role in student dishonesty means to take a stance for what he believes to be core values they as faculty should embody, despite the danger of offending some of his colleagues.

Question Discussion

1. In the combined role as faculty member and researcher, how can one build trust to engage students in honest responses regarding their potential dishonest behavior?
2. How can assessments of dishonesty be optimally framed in the sense of engaging students in discourse and raising awareness instead of confronting or condemning them about their behavior?
3. What role does the student-teacher relationship play in cheating behavior on assessments?

Conclusion

Researchers of academic dishonesty who simultaneously teach students at university have to consider the importance of trust when assessing dishonest behavior of the students.

Case 10: Using Relational Coordination to Promote Academic Integrity

Matt Rahimian, Huron at Western University, Canada

Synopsis/Summary

When Matt started a job as an academic integrity officer, he soon realized how vast the domain of the role is and how limited the resources are. The dilemma for him to resolve was to convince various stakeholders to invest in academic integrity initiatives. Besides an existing policy, few leverages existed to initiate an academic integrity culture change.

Applying innovative approaches to promote academic integrity seemed inevitable, yet how far could one go with such innovative approaches?

Supporting Information

A few years ago, Matt was employed as an academic integrity officer at a post-secondary institution. He was invited to talk in new faculty training sessions. In the six sessions he attended, he experienced different opinions on academic integrity, from welcoming relevant initiatives to accepting it as a failed battle. In one of the sessions, Julie said: "I think it is a lost war . . . with all the sharing websites, social media group chats, and other cheating tools, I think we have already lost that battle." Matt remembered that in other sessions, several faculty members shared techniques they had used to promote academic integrity in their courses. He contemplated the complexity of the issues. Not only was there little leverage to create compliance, but there were diverging approaches to the prospects and possibilities of the matter.

After being employed at a different post-secondary institution as an academic integrity coordinator, he realized similar dilemmas of diverging attitudes and the challenge of compliance. While some faculties were seeking ways to develop a module to educate students on those issues, Matt informed them that a well-constructed module had been designed by one of the units and has been in use for some time. This made him realize that a disconnect had caused some challenges.

Value Discussion

The primary value addressed in this case study is trust. From his discussion with some faculty members, Matt realized the issues might be rooted in the element of trust. In this example, had Julie trusted the system, she would have asked her colleagues how to promote academic integrity and prevent cheating, or if she had discussed her concerns with Matt, she would have learned how to promote academic integrity. If trust is being implemented among colleagues at an institution and between various departments, it would be possible to resolve some of the daily challenges of academic integrity practitioners.

Fairness is one of the secondary values discussed in this case study. Would it be fair for some students taking Course A with Instructor X to *earn* their credentials while another group of students taking the same course with Instructor Y *cheat* their way through their studies? One requirement to maintain academic integrity is responding to departures from academic integrity consistently (ICAI, 2021, p. 7). While it may not obliterate the academic integrity challenges, collaborating with others to learn from their effective practices to promote academic integrity and later integrate those practices into our work can facilitate fairness through sustaining academic integrity.

Respect is another secondary value described in this case study. When seeking advice from our colleagues to promote academic integrity, we acknowledge their work and experiences. Building coordinated teams would create a community that respects each member's opinions which can vary from each other. These attempts would promote respect for students' credentials at our institutions. When an environment of respect is created, the chances of students' respecting their work and the work of others are increased.

Working in academic environments, we take responsibility for educating our students with integrity. The responsibility that Matt could see was one for him and all his colleagues and beyond them in their institution. The dominant onus is on the faculty to educate students, whether that is an education on specific subjects or on how to maintain their work integrity. Therefore, investments in actions to promote academic integrity is an act of taking responsibility. Through collaborations with colleagues in and out of their institutions, academic integrity practitioners and faculty members take responsibility for promoting academic integrity. However, the dilemma persists as not all staff, including faculty members, are committed to taking responsibility for promoting academic integrity.

Question Discussion

1. How can we promote trust by adapting an educational approach?
2. How can practitioners promote fairness, respect, and responsibility through creating collaborative teams?
3. What are the challenges of promoting trust, fairness, and responsibility as integral elements of academic integrity in post-secondary education?

Conclusion

Building trust among various units in an institution is fundamental to not only learning from each other how to promote academic integrity but also to practicing fairness, respect, and responsibility.

References

Bolton, R., Logan, C., and Gittell, J. H. "Revisiting relational coordination: A systematic review." *The Journal of Applied Behavioral Science,* 57, no. 3, 290–322, 2021. DOI: org/10.1177/0021886321991597

Woolfolk, A. E., Winne, P. H., and Perry, N. E. *Educational Psychology* (5th Canadian edition), 2021. Toronto, Canada: Pearson.

Case 11: Telling Family Secrets

Claude E. P. Mayo, Quinnipiac University, United States

Synopsis/Summary

Phil is the academic integrity administrator at Jerome University in the United States. While investigating a case, the accused student claims that the faculty member involved has shared information about that case with her stepson. The student, who once lived with that same stepson, now posits that the confidentiality breach has compromised the adjudication process, his reputation, and FERPA. The accused student produces three witnesses—all alumni—who attest to learning about the academic integrity case from the stepson.

Supporting Information

While investigating the report submitted by a faculty member, Phil, the lead academic integrity administrator at Jerome University, receives a response from the accused student claiming impropriety in the present case. In relatively detailed claims, the student explains with relative certainty that a breach of confidentiality has shared personal information relative to his participation in the process throughout the school community. Additionally, the student raises his concern about how this breach has implications for violating FERPA rights.

To corroborate his allegations, the student has provided the contact information for three people who have received direct knowledge of the private information about his adjudication. Each of the students is a recent alumnus of the university and has significant prior connections—i.e., fraternity brother, friend, roommate—to the accused student. When Phil reaches out to confirm the story of each of these witnesses, each is willing to talk and share an account similar to the students.

Potentially the most concerning part of the breach of confidentiality allegations for Phil is that the student believes that the information was shared by the reporting faculty member. The student claims to have run into the faculty member's stepson recently when the stepson asked "Are you OK? I mean from the academic integrity stuff." The student knows the faculty member's stepson as the two were once roommates at Jerome University and still socialize in circles that often overlap and include the three witnesses offered by the student.

Value Discussion

The primary value for this case is trust. The academic integrity process relies on all parties being truthful to arrive at the true and best result for the academic community. In this situation, allegations about the process itself being compromised rely upon conflicting stories about what information may have been shared outside of the process. At the same time, it is difficult to determine whether the compromising behavior did in fact take place and so the investigation into whether it did will inevitably rely upon who the academic integrity officer can trust is telling the truth.

A secondary value for this case is fairness. In trying to determine how to proceed, Phil must determine and stay resolute on a process that is objective and consistent with the rules relative to all parties. The original case remains at the core of this academic integrity matter but there is certainly another—breach of confidentiality—that will need to be resolved beforehand. And if that breach is found to have occurred, there could be implications for the academic integrity case (can it continue?), the faculty member responsible for it (any sanction necessary?), and even the institution (any FERPA liability?).

Question Discussion

1. How should Phil consider the merit of and investigate the breach of confidentiality claims against the faculty member within this case?
2. What are the stakeholder perspectives that Phil needs to consider as he concludes his investigation and continues the adjudication of the potential academic integrity violation? What makes those perspectives most salient?
3. How should an academic integrity investigation, adjudication, and resolution consider and accommodate potentially compromising information external to its process?
4. How should the academic integrity board members be informed and/or instructed to consider the potential breach of confidentiality?
5. When, if ever, should Phil share this scenario with other departments and/or university administrators? Please explain with which departments/individuals and why.

Conclusion

Trust is necessary to navigate the many external circumstances—including confidentiality and personal relationships—that can complicate and potentially compromise the investigation, adjudication, and resolution of potential academic integrity violations.

Case 12: What Do You Mean Students Are in Charge?

Jason T. Ciejka and Blaire N. Wilson, Emory University, United States

Synopsis/Summary

The president of the University Faculty Senate has asked the senate to consider making changes to the student-governed honor system. She was disappointed that a student she reported for academic misconduct was not found responsible by the student honor council and believes that faculty must be on the hearing boards with voting power. There is much discussion among faculty about whether to trust the process as is or whether to intervene in the honor system and add a faculty role.

Supporting Information

Decatur University has a longstanding student-initiated and -led honor code. Student honor council members are the sole decision makers in reported cases, although there is oversight from the academic integrity office.

Professor Haygood, who teaches economics and serves as the president of the University Faculty Senate, reported a student for cheating on a final exam in the spring semester after she found a crib sheet underneath the student's chair. The student honor council determined that the crib sheet was in fact an agenda for the student's plan for studying; it had slipped from her pocket during the exam and there were no clear links between the agenda, which had little content, and the student's responses on the test.

Professor Haygood was furious when she learned of the decision to find the student not responsible. She believes that there should be a formal faculty voice in the decisions of the honor council.

At the first meeting of the University Faculty Senate, she proposes a motion to include a faculty vote on honor council hearings arguing, "We cannot leave these important decisions about guilt and innocence in the hands of students alone. How can they possibly make appropriate decisions involving their peers without our faculty to guide them?" Although a contingent of faculty members agree with Professor Haygood, others argue that students at the university have long made these decisions, and the faculty should not change course based on a single unfavorable verdict.

Value Discussion

Trust is the primary value within this case. When faculty report cases of academic dishonesty, they place trust in academic integrity offices, boards, and honor councils to make fair and appropriate decisions. Processes that incorporate student board members or student honor councils may require even greater trust among the faculty, and institutions should actively cultivate that trust. A single decision can erode trust if the institution does not communicate in a transparent way or work to help the faculty understand the decision and respond, in turn, to legitimate concerns.

Fairness is one of the secondary values seen in this case. Reporting faculty may at times disagree with decisions by academic integrity boards and honor councils. The fact that boards and honor councils do not reach foregone conclusions helps demonstrate that these processes are fair and reported students can expect their cases to be reviewed in a fair and impartial manner. Students, faculty, and staff bring different perspectives to cases. Articulating how a decision is based on a rational foundation tied firmly to evidence will help alleviate concerns an individual faculty may have about a single decision.

Another secondary value in this case is responsibility. The reporting faculty member's concerns about the academic integrity process and willingness to address them in the forum of the University Faculty Senate shows a shared responsibility over academic integrity at the institution. Rather than jumping to the conclusion that the process needs to be reformed, this situation could have been an opportunity for the academic integrity office to share more information with the individual faculty and the University Faculty Senate as a whole about the honor code process.

Question Discussion

1. How do institutions help faculty understand that a fair process means that there will be some decisions they disagree with?
2. How do students and faculty work together to have meaningful conversations about academic integrity processes?
3. How do governance structures and administrative structures impact academic integrity policies?

Conclusion

The success of any academic integrity policy relies on the trust that stakeholders, including students and faculty, place in it.

Chapter 3
Fairness

Chapter Contents:

All for One and One for All
  Greg Preston, University of Newcastle, Australia
Collusion by Coercion
  Emma J. Thacker, University of Toronto, Canada and Angela Clark, York University, Canada
It's Not My Problem Until It's Been Turned In
  Jason T. Ciejka and Blaire N. Wilson, Emory University, United States
Higher Learning, Higher Stakes
  Sara Kellogg, Iowa State University, United States
Collusion Confusion
  Courtney Cullen, University of Georgia, United States
It Doesn't Add Up
  Claude E. P. Mayo, Quinnipiac University, United States
Can't Put My Finger on It
  Claude E. P. Mayo, Quinnipiac University, United States
Multi-use Presentations, "Retritos"
  Edna Orta-Anes, Universidad Ana G. Mendez-Recinto de Gurabo, Puerto Rico
Procedural Empathy
  Joshua Wolf, Elaine Currie, and Jeremy Bourgoin, Vanderbilt University, United States
Flagrant Foul on the Faculty
  Blaire N. Wilson and Jason T. Ciejka, Emory University, United States
Towards Fair and Balanced Budgeting
  Greer Murphy, University of Rochester, United States

Socialize with Specialists to Spot and Stem Spinning
  Abby Pfeiffer, Heather Frase, Katie Frank, Ben McDermott, and Kacy Vargas,
  Western Governors University, United States

Fairness is focusing on impartial treatment or looking at bias making sure you understand where your biases are associated with this fair or impartial treatment. Fairness emphasizes and reinforces those values of truth within logic and rationality. Fairness can be seen by making sure that the ideas of the rules, policies, and procedures are applied consistently as it applies both to the institution, faculty member, and student. Engaging with others equitably ensures you keep an open mind, taking responsibility for your own actions. A faculty leads by example making sure to uphold those principles associated with the fairness principle and to communicate those expectations as we go through the academic year making sure that the institution has clear, useful, and consistent policies and that there is a degree of transparency.

There are 12 case studies in this book which address the primary value of fairness.

Case Studies Focused on the Student. There are four case studies which primarily address the student perspective.

Three of the cases address group assignments. In "Case 1: *All for One and One for All*" three students submit a paper in which a section of the work from one student has significant unacknowledged matches to a previously published journal article. The students who did not plagiarize their sections maintain that they should not be penalized for the conduct of another person. In "Case 2: *Collusion by Coercion*" a student is upset about a penalty she received for participating in collusion since she was intimidated into committing the academic misconduct. In "Case 3: *It's Not My Problem Until It's Been Turned In*" a group member who is doing the final proofreading notices that one of the sections of the paper written by another member includes heavy plagiarism. She writes to the professor to ask for help and advice about the situation.

The final case study addressing the student perspective deals with a graduate student. In "Case 4: *Higher Learning, Higher Stakes*" a graduate student submits a paper for draft review. The reviewing professor found uncited content and confronted the student stating there are higher expectations for graduate student work.

Case Studies Focused on the Faculty and/or Administrator. There are six case studies which primarily address this perspective.

Three of the cases address testing issues. In "Case 5: *Collusion Confusion*" students had an open-note take-home exam. However, some students posted the answers on a third-party website and identified collusion among some of the students. In "Case 6: *It Doesn't Add Up*" a student borrowed a roommate's calculator midway through the latest examination. In "Case 7: *Can't Put My Finger on It*" while reviewing online examination submissions, a faculty member found that a student made an obscene hand gesture to the camera during a preliminary identification phase of the exercise. The faculty was so offended that she refused to grade the examination, assigned the student a zero, and submitted the incident to the campus academic integrity authority.

One case addresses reuse of previously submitted work. In "Case 8: *Multi-use Presentations, 'Retritos'*" a faculty member noticed that the delivered presentation had the title of the assigned topic but the name of another professor and the title and code of another course which was a violation of school policy.

One case addresses a situation where the student does not have the skills necessary to submit the assignment. In "Case 9: *Procedural Empathy*" a faculty member accused a student of plagiarism on her first paper in a college setting. The student admits to improperly citing her sources and adds that she has never written a research paper before, so she did not know how to create citations.

The final case study from the faculty perspective addresses inconsistent treatment of students. In "Case 10: *Flagrant Foul on the Faculty*" the dean received complaints from students accused of plagiarism that student athletes were simply given the opportunity to resubmit their assignments.

Case Studies Focused on the Academic Integrity Office and Authenticity Team. The remaining two case studies primarily address this perspective.

In "Case 11: *Towards Fair and Balanced Budgeting*" the integrity officer proposes a budget to address the increased consultation requests and tripled cases. She only received 25 percent of her request, and she is not sure how to proceed since starting incrementally on both areas seems counterproductive but targeting one at the expense of the other seems unfair.

In "Case 12: *Socialize with Specialists to Spot and Stem Spinning*" the academic authenticity team is asked to evaluate a submission which has been suspected of being spun. The emphasis is on cross-department collaboration to determine if this is an authenticity or a writing issue, in order to customize student support.

In addition to the 12 case studies in this chapter on fairness, 25 other case studies in this book address fairness as a secondary value. Refer to that value chapter as shown for an introduction to each case study.

Trust:

- *Telling Family Secrets*
- *Clear as . . . Mud*
- *Reduce, Reuse, Recycle*
- *Suspicious Success*
- *What Do You Mean Students Are in Charge?*
- *Pressure vs. Courage: The Dean's Dilemma*
- *Using Relational Coordination to Promote Academic Integrity*

Honesty:

- *Should I Pay the Contract Cheating Sites to Get the Answer?*
- *Readied Recalcitrance*

Respect:

- *The Emotional Rollercoaster of Reporting*
- *Punishment and Rehabilitation*
- *Personalized and Supportive Proctoring Processes*
- *Tipping the Scale: Mental Health and Outcomes*
- *Advising Not Policing: Respecting the Students*

Responsibility:

- *Does Co-Authorship Imply a Responsibility for the Whole Document?*
- *Fake Grade Booster Classes*
- *Weighing the Options*
- *Scaffolding Writing for an A*
- *That's Not Fair: Balancing the Workload for Remote Teams*
- *Student's Legal Defense and Institutional Responsibility*
- *Statistically Surprising Standardized State-Wide Scores Sold*

Courage:

- *Mock Police Board Exam Puts Students in the Hot Seat*
- *To Pursue or Not Pursue*
- *Taking a Stand for Integrity: A Whistleblower's Tale*
- *Demonstrating Courage to Stand for Integrity*

Case 1: All for One and One for All

Greg Preston, University of Newcastle, Australia

Synopsis/Summary

A group of three students submit a group project consisting of a paper and a class presentation in a first-year history course at an Australian university. A section of the work has significant unacknowledged matches to a previously published journal article. A preliminary discussion with the group identifies that one student has plagiarized significant sections of their submission. The students who did not plagiarize their sections maintain that they should not be penalized for the conduct of another person, however the academic is uncomfortable with allowing any students to benefit from work that is in breach of academic standards.

Supporting Information

Pat, Sally, and April are all students undertaking a first-year history course at an Australian university. As part of the assessment for the course students have been asked to complete a group project as part of their work on "Social change in response to World War One." The project has two parts: a class presentation and written paper. The students decide to divide the content into three sections with each student responsible for their own section of the paper and for producing the slides for the presentation on their content area. All the students complete their sections independently and then "assemble" the final presentation and paper at a group meeting.

Following the presentation, the course coordinator, Dr. Smyth, asks to speak to the students. She indicates that their paper has been flagged by the university's text matching software and that it appears that some of the material presented in the paper has been copied from an online journal article without any attribution. As the discussion progresses it becomes clear that the section of work that is causing concern has been prepared by Pat. Pat indicates that she was under pressure and did copy from the article to complete her section of the assignment.

All three students are now worried about how their marks for this course will be affected. The course coordinator discusses with Pat the possibility of redoing their section of the assignment. Pat indicates that she intends to drop the course. April and Sally are now concerned that they will have to do more work than their classmates because of the actions of another student.

Value Discussion

The case study primarily investigates the concept of fairness through staff and students exploring the relationship between individual progress and group assignments. The dimensions here include the possibility of students who have not engaged in problematic behavior being impacted by the behavior of another student and balancing that against the fairness of those same individuals being advantaged by "wrong" behavior. The issue of fairness is played out both within the group being specifically investigated and the relationship of this group with the wider cohort.

The case study addresses honesty in group work situations as a secondary value. It relates to the foundational importance of honesty in the development of trust within groups, and the development of processes within group work patterns to ensure the development of lifelong integrity. Faculty and student management of groups to ensure honesty can be addressed through this case study.

Responsibility is also a secondary value addressed in this case study as it explores dimensions of personal responsibility. Additionally, the scenario considers the way that individual actions can impact the academic progression of others. There are opportunities to explore the responsibilities of individuals within group activities both within tasks generally, and in relation to material that is assessed.

Question Discussion

1. What options are open to the academic in this case?
2. Is it reasonable that a student should be rewarded for plagiarized work, or punished for the misdeeds of others in their group?
3. What instructions or changes to a group assignment could be made to minimize these issues in the future?

Conclusion

The notion of fairness in terms of appropriate penalties is extremely complex in cases where group work is involved.

Case 2: Collusion by Coercion

Emma J. Thacker, University of Toronto, Canada and Angela Clark, York University, Canada

Synopsis/Summary

Jennifer is a first-year undergraduate student. Jennifer has come to the university ombudsperson office and is very upset about a penalty she received for participating in collusion: she had completed work for classmates which they submitted as their own. Jennifer believes that the penalty she received is unfair because she was intimidated into committing the academic misconduct. She seeks the ombudsperson's assistance and asks whether this penalty can be reduced.

Supporting Information

JENNIFER:	There are two guys in my class from my hometown. They are both lazy and they know that I work hard for my good grades. A few weeks back they cornered me and threatened that if I didn't do the next assignment for both of them, they would tell everyone back home that I sleep around. I was terrified, as I know that my family would be ashamed and devastated. It would cause a lot of humiliation, and I may not be able to come back to school. So, I did my own assignment, then changed some wording and sent them each a different version.
THE OMBUDSPERSON:	I'm sorry to hear this, Jennifer. Can you tell me what happened next?

JENNIFER: I was incredibly busy and stressed out,
and I guess I didn't change one ver-
sion enough. The instructor noticed
that the assignment I handed in was
very similar to the assignment I did
for one of the guys. I was too scared
to tell my instructor what really happened. So, we both received a penalty
of a failing grade in the course. The
other student got away with it. I am
very worried about my GPA, the tui-
tion I paid, and I'm also worried that
the student will come after me for getting him into trouble. How can I get
the penalty reduced and stay safe?

Value Discussion

The primary value for this case study is fairness. Students demonstrate fairness when they complete their own work and respect academic
integrity policies, and institutionally, fairness is demonstrated when
misconduct is addressed in a consistent manner (ICAI, 2021, p. 7). This
case shows that to ensure equitable outcomes, fair treatment does not
always involve consistent treatment. The male students disregarded fairness by bullying Jennifer into completing their work, not only defying
academic integrity expectations, but victimizing another student as well.
Due to fear, Jennifer complied, and did not disclose the truth when questioned. The decision maker, acting impartially on the information they
had, imposed the same penalty for two students.

Responsibility is a secondary value which means taking a stand
against wrongdoing (ICAI, 2021, p. 9). Jennifer did not provide her
instructor with the full story when academic misconduct was suspected.
The two male students also did not report what happened when given
the opportunity to take responsibility. Jennifer had her reasons: she
feared repercussions for herself and for her family's reputation. Eventually, she did seek out the ombudsperson's assistance and during their
meeting, she recounted exactly what had happened. In this way, Jennifer
took responsibility for the collusion and furthermore, revealed that she
was a victim of threatening and inappropriate behavior.

Question Discussion

1. Can new information support the review of an academic misconduct penalty by the decision maker? What should the student consider?
2. What is the ombudsperson's role in this case?
3. Should Jennifer's penalty be reconsidered in light of the new information?
4. What student support services can be engaged to support the students through the resolution of the case, and beyond?
5. What about the second student who had not received an allegation? Should he now be investigated, or is that unfair?

Conclusion

This case presents the complexities of the student experience and demonstrates that to achieve fairness, each case must be considered on its own merits, and include consideration for extenuating circumstances and students' intersectional experience.

References

International Center for Academic Integrity [ICAI]. (2021). The Fundamental Values of Academic Integrity, 3rd ed., 2021. https://academicintegrity.org/images/pdfs/20019_ICAI-Fundamental-Values_R12.pdf

Ombudsman Saskatchewan. "What is fairness?," 2019. https://ombudsman.sk.ca/app/uploads/2020/01/What-is-Fairness-Jan-2019.pdf

Sutherland Smith, W. *Plagiarism, the internet and student learning: Improving Academic Integrity*. Routledge, 2008.

Case 3: It's Not My Problem Until It's Been Turned In

Jason T. Ciejka and Blaire N. Wilson, Emory University, United States

Synopsis/Summary

A couple hours before the deadline for a group paper, a group member who is doing the final proofreading notices that one of the sections of the paper written by another member includes heavy plagiarism. She writes to the professor to ask for help and advice about the situation. The professor responds that the paper is due in two hours, and if any part is plagiarized, she will report the group to the academic integrity office.

Supporting Information

Farah and her group members have been working on the research project for their psychology class all semester. Farah, in particular, has taken the lead in managing the project and keeping her teammates organized and on track. Although the group has worked collaboratively throughout the process, the students decided on a divide-and-conquer approach to the main write-up. Each of the four members has taken on the task of writing one of the four main sections of the paper.

The group has been sharing drafts in the weeks leading up to the final deadline. The afternoon the paper is due, Farah does one final proofread of the paper, but suddenly has a nagging suspicion that one of the sections may have some plagiarized passages. A search on the internet confirms this is the case. Farah reaches out to her group members but doesn't hear back and remembers that they're all taking final exams for other classes that afternoon.

With the deadline just a couple hours away, she sends an urgent message to Professor Gupta asking for guidance about how to handle the situation. Professor Gupta responds, "I'm sorry to hear about this situation. In fairness to the whole class, I cannot offer you an extension. The deadline for the paper is in two hours. I hope you'll be able to correct any issues with plagiarism and citation before then. As a faculty member, I will have a duty to report any plagiarized work to the academic integrity office, so I hope you can address this now."

Value Discussion

The primary value in this case is fairness. Questions about fairness often surface when a faculty member has a clear and reasonable policy, such as the deadline for a paper, but a student presents compelling reasons for an exception. Faculty may naturally question how to respond to such requests in a way that is fair. What does it mean to offer consistent and transparent application of policies when there may be individual circumstances that are compelling and require deeper consideration and possibly a deviation from the established policies? Within group projects, what is a fair expectation for authorship and duty of other group members to ensure originality.

Question Discussion

1. What is the responsibility of an individual student to ensure that group members are practicing academic integrity?
2. How can faculty provide support and guidance to students when a student is concerned about possible academic misconduct?
3. What is a fair way to handle such a situation that does not penalize or potentially harm the honest student for reporting her concerns?

Conclusion

The issue of fairness often surfaces in group work, and instructors should consider how to respond to concerns about group dynamics and academic integrity to promote a fair playing field.

Case 4: Higher Learning, Higher Stakes

Sara Kellogg, Iowa State University, United States

Synopsis/Summary

Lee submits a graduate level research paper draft at an American accredited University for required review. The reviewing professor found uncited content and confronted Lee. Lee shared the paper was a draft so citations were not finalized but he can provide the list of works used. The professor indicates a higher expectation for graduate student work and informs Lee he will be referred to the student conduct office for plagiarism and academic penalty.

Supporting Information

Lee is a graduate student pursuing a master's degree in educational administration. Lee's supervising faculty, Dr. Chan, has requested Lee submit the most recent draft of a research paper for midterm review. While reading Lee's paper, Dr. Chan recognizes some of the content to be from a published journal article, but without citation. After confirming the attribution, Dr. Chan asks Lee to meet. He shares his suspicion of plagiarism and asks Lee to explain.

Lee appears surprised by the allegation and states, "You wanted to see a draft of my paper, but it isn't finalized, so it doesn't include all my references." Lee goes on to explain, "With my writing style, I typically just make myself a note and add references at the end." Lee adds that if Dr. Chan doesn't believe him, he can share the list of all the works he used. Dr. Chan remains unimpressed, and responds, "As a graduate student, any work you submit for review is expected to be of a high standard of quality. Even drafts at this level are expected to have clear citations so that these can be assessed for appropriate inclusion." Dr. Chan informs Lee that students should never submit anything, draft or not, where they present information from another source as their own. Dr. Chan shares that the situation will be referred to the student conduct office for review for plagiarism and an academic penalty will be discussed with the department chair.

Value Discussion

Fairness is the primary value within this case. All students must ensure attribution for any external sources and acknowledge when work is borrowed in any coursework submitted. Faculty may be unable or unwilling to excuse violations of certain academic standards and must apply expectations in a consistent and fair manner.

Both responsibility and honesty can be seen as secondary values in this case. Students should always endeavor to submit high quality work and clarify questions about course expectations proactively, understanding it is their responsibility to perform at the level expected of all students. Faculty have a responsibility to clearly communicate academic expectations and guidelines and to determine the most appropriate response where students appear to have had honest intentions.

Question Discussion

1. Should graduate students be expected to perform at higher standards, even for draft work submitted?

2. How much consideration should be given to the student's explanation for their actions?

3. Does the faculty's response in this case seem to be influenced by anything other than the facts of the situation?

4. Are there certain unwritten policies, expectations, or standards that students should be held accountable to no matter what?

Conclusion

Students must be accountable for their academic work and meeting expectations therefore faculty are called to have a fair standard of expectations and assessments.

Case 5: Collusion Confusion

Courtney Cullen, University of Georgia, United States

Synopsis/Summary

Dr. Plum provided a take-home exam for a data sciences course that was open note, but stated that students could not work together. However, some students posted the answers on a third-party website. Because Dr. Plum was checking to see which student posted the exam question, they dove into the LMS data of the exams and found what looked like collusion between many of the students during the exam. Now Dr. Plum has over 200 cases of potential dishonesty in their course.

Supporting Information

Dr. Plum opened the third online, take-home exam of the semester on Tuesday with the following instructions at the top:

> You have until Thursday at 11:59 p.m. to complete your exam. You are allowed to use the slides from lecture and any personal notes that you have taken to complete the exam. You are not allowed to access a tutor or online tutoring service or discuss any exam questions with any other individual.

The following day, Dr. Plum heard a colleague complain about students posting test questions online, so they decided to Google the questions to see if any popped up. They found exam questions posted to an online "helping" site with the answers for all three exams given during the semester. They contacted the integrity office and asked for help getting the questions removed and finding out who posted and viewed the questions. The report that was returned included 18 unique users but did not have names for all of the posters and viewers. The report did list IP addresses and other timestamped information.

In order to identify the unnamed students and report them to the integrity office, Dr. Plum had to dig through the exam data from each exam on the online learning management system (LMS). Once they had all of the data, they started noticing some patterns of other students submitting answers at the exact same time. Dr. Plum ran an analysis to find which students took exams at the same time. They were dismayed to find that nearly 200 students had taken exams in groups ranging in size from two to six students. Further digging into the data showed that not only were they completing the exam at the exact same time, but they were answering questions that were in a randomized order at the exact same time as well.

Value Discussion

The primary value in this case is fairness. Dr. Plum needs to be fair to the students that completed the work honestly. They must address the cheating that occurred, otherwise there is no incentive to be honest moving forward. They also need to be fair to the different types and levels of collusion that occurred on the test in deciding punishments. What makes an equitable sanction for the students that posted the questions online versus the students that worked together at the end of the test to double-check their answers? Dr. Plum must follow university expectations to report all of the students potentially involved and listen to their explanations with an open mind.

A secondary value is responsibility. Dr. Plum has the responsibility to report the students that posted exam questions to the third-party tutoring site *and* the students that colluded on the assignment. They need to have conversations with the students about their actions and the consequences of those actions. Not only is reporting a part of the institutional policy, but it also contributes to a culture of integrity on campus.

Dr. Plum also has the responsibility to restore integrity to their course and exams moving forward. How they address the issue now can help develop their course in the future.

Another secondary value is honesty. Students should be honest in their work by completing the exam independently. For the students that were not honest on the exam, they now have an opportunity to be honest with Dr. Plum by providing a truthful account of what happened during the exam. If they were in discussion, even if the discussion was held remotely, they have colluded on the exam. Dr. Plum should be honest with the class about the impacts of this cheating behavior, both in terms of the course and the emotional toll and overall workload increase that the cheating has caused.

Question Discussion

1. What are the ethics of ignoring some types of cheating, but not others?
2. How can administration and faculty work together in large scale cases of academic dishonesty?
3. As a faculty member, what strategies can Professor Plum utilize to restore the integrity in their classroom?

Conclusion

What may seem like a simple case of cheating can easily become more complex and time consuming but being fair and consistent in dealing with cheating in the classroom is instrumental to building a culture of integrity.

Case 6: It Doesn't Add Up

Claude E. P. Mayo, Quinnipiac University, United States

Synopsis/Summary

While updating his academic advisor Nick on science course progress, a student shared that he borrowed a roommate's calculator midway through the latest examination. The student did not share whether the professor was aware, but Nick knows that campus academic integrity prohibits "Using unauthorized materials or the assistance of an unauthorized person." When the academic integrity officer investigates further, the professor did not know and does not think this behavior helped on the examination.

Supporting Information

Partway through their regular advising meeting, Nick's student mentions that he struggled on a recent science examination but was lucky because he was able to "borrow" his roommate's calculator when his died during the examination. The student "would have been screwed" if not for borrowing the calculator at that time.

Nick became instantly concerned about whether this use of another student's calculator violated the academic integrity policy. Nick's research of the policy revealed that "[u]sing unauthorized materials or the assistance of an unauthorized person" is a violation but he was still confused as to whether this occurred. Nick did not know what, if any, information was transferred with the calculator nor how to interpret the student's use of the word "borrow" to indicate whether the roommate willingly handed over the calculator or his student took it off the other student's desk when that student finished the examination. Nick reported the information he had to the academic integrity office on campus.

The academic integrity officer hoped to gain some clarity about the situation by reaching out to the professor since the report did not originate from the class itself. The faculty member was shocked to hear that the calculator transfer had transpired during the examination as he was completely unaware of it. But he was also not concerned as he did not think that the calculator—regardless of its source—provided any additional advantage to the student. The professor said that if he was aware of the student's calculator dying during the examination, he would have lent the student his own calculator.

Value Discussion

The primary value described in this case study is fairness. Each academic integrity violation—and the process that seeks to determine it—should be purely motivated by the best intentions of the community hosting it. The community in this discussion is potentially split as the faculty does not recognize an advantage deriving from the student's behavior while Nick recognizes behavior that clearly extends beyond the guidelines established by the policy. The Office of Academic Integrity must reconcile the situation between these sides while establishing a precedent that will hold in the future.

The secondary value described in this case study is responsibility. Each character in this scenario has a terrific opportunity to be responsible for maintaining the academic community of the institution. Nick, upon learning this new but incomplete information, has accepted his duty to investigate and report a potential violation in the community. His student has the opportunity to recognize controversial behavior under the policy and accept responsibility for the violation; the other student—as a facilitator and/or knowledgeable party—can as well. Lastly the academic integrity administrator must honor the office's duty to simultaneously uphold the policy while supporting the faculty members it seeks to protect.

Question Discussion

1. Should the student's behavior initiate an academic integrity violation case under this section of the academic integrity violation?
2. If an academic integrity case is initiated, should the student be found responsible or not responsible for the violation? Why?
3. Should an academic integrity case be initiated against the second student whose calculator was borrowed? Are there any circumstances or factors that cause this answer to switch?
4. To what extent should the faculty member's lack of concern about the behavior lead to a non-start/dismissal of the academic integrity case?

Conclusion

Some behavior(s) and circumstances cause conflict between the letter and spirit of academic integrity policy; institutions must resolve conflicts with clear and consistent standards for fairness throughout the academic community.

Case 7: Can't Put My Finger on It

Claude E. P. Mayo, Quinnipiac University, United States

Synopsis/Summary

Grace is a math faculty member at a medium-sized US university. While reviewing online examination submissions, she found that a student made an obscene hand gesture to the camera during a preliminary identification phase of the exercise. Grace was so offended that she refused to grade the examination, assigned the student a zero, and submitted the incident to the campus academic integrity authority. The student contested the assigned grade and therefore refused to accept responsibility for the behavior as a violation.

Supporting Information

In the university's online testing system, before a student enters the question part of an examination, the student must both show their face in full and produce their school identification card for identification purposes. During a recent examination, this math student added his middle finger to the interchange between the two requests. Grace was so offended upon seeing the action—which she perceived as clearly directed towards her through the camera—that she aborted grading the examination and assigned the student a zero grade.

Grace is unsure what, if anything else, she should do upon finding the student's action. She immediately consults with a colleague who encourages her to think of the behavior as "a violation of the student Code of Conduct because it is so rude; how could a student behave like that?" In defining the purpose of the academic integrity policy, Grace's colleague remarked that it should be focused squarely on "students' academic behavior in the classroom to prevent cheating and plagiarism" which this student's action was not.

However Grace was not convinced that this situation escaped violating academic integrity. Grace debated whether this behavior fit within another type of violation—Interfering with the Academic Community—included in the university policy. So despite contacting the Office of Student Conduct as the colleague advised, Grace simultaneously reported the student's behavior to the Office of Academic Integrity for full follow-up there as well.

The university academic integrity policy outlined a judicial process that began with the report, called for a student response, and then included a board hearing of the charge. The policy is silent on how an assignment is to be graded—if at all—while it is being challenged and investigated on academic integrity grounds.

Value Discussion

Fairness is the primary value described in this case study. It is a necessary consideration for both the faculty member's and student's perspective and protection. Whether the policy is being interpreted beyond its bounds to include behavior that does not have a direct impact on academic work must be determined to protect the student from an extraneous academic integrity charge. Similarly, whether the policy protects the faculty member from disrespectful treatment by a student outside of the public view of others but in a virtual classroom setting is essential to know.

Both Grace and the student have significant responsibility to each other and the university community. While the student did attest to the inappropriateness of the recorded action, the student has refused to take responsibility for that action because of the pre-academic integrity process sanction that Grace has applied. Meanwhile Grace's behavior of taking a judicial-like action prior to initiating the academic integrity process may not be upholding her duty as a faculty member.

Question Discussion

1. Should Grace's concern and subsequent report about the student's action initiate the academic integrity violation process, a student conduct policy violation process, or both for appropriate resolution?
2. What are the pros and cons of the student's act of performing an obscene hand gesture before participating in an examination being determined to be a violation of the academic integrity code?
3. Can Grace refuse to grade and assign a zero grade to the student's examination in response to conduct she believes will be determined a violation of the academic integrity code?

4. How might the Office of Academic Integrity advise the student relative to the faculty member assigning a zero grade as separate from the conduct which potentially violated the campus code?

Conclusion

Determining fair academic integrity processes and outcomes for students can be difficult when broad policy language enables discretion in covering non-academic conduct and determining appropriate faculty responses to potential violations.

Case 8: Multi-use Presentations, "Retritos"

Edna Orta-Anes, Universidad Ana G. Mendez-Recinto de Gurabo, Puerto Rico

Synopsis/Summary

William and Israel were assigned to develop the Business Ethics topic and make a presentation in class. The faculty member noticed that the delivered presentation had the title of the assigned topic but the name of another professor and the title and code of another course. The students are notified of the issue. They are told that what they had done was a violation of school policy.

Supporting Information

In the Organizational Behavior course, students are assigned a topic to develop in a report and make a class presentation. The students must start meeting as a group, divide the work, prepare an outline to hand in the third week of classes. In addition to the presentation, they must prepare a three-page narrative related to the topic. Groups are expected to develop their topics by aligning them with the main theme of the course.

Since the course will be offered online, students are instructed that they must deliver their presentation half an hour before classes begin, so that the teacher can upload it on the platform. Upon reviewing the one submitted by William and Israel, the faculty member notices that it has a cover that indicates the assigned topic title, but the name and code of another course as well as the name of another professor. The faculty member makes a copy and uploads it to the virtual classroom after removing the information about the other course and the other teacher. She wrote in the comments section "There will be repercussions for this situation, you tried to upload this work four times without even trying to hide that you used it for another course."

Israel sent an e-mail message saying "This morning I saw the message you put in the presentation assignment for Workshop #5. I apologize if this fact offended you. My colleague William and I shared the task, and it was a mistake on his part when he prepared the PowerPoint presentation. The blame also falls on me because I did not pay attention to the reference to another course when uploading the presentation to the platform. I feel bad about this situation. Sorry again if I offended you. I uploaded the presentation again this morning with the error corrected. Sincerely, Israel."

William never reacted.

Value Discussion

The primary value described in this case study is fairness. Faculty members should project an impartial position when dealing with students. Our expectation for the students' appropriate behavior and performance as well as the rules and procedures to enforce it, should be established for each instructional task and activity. We cannot let a deviation from these established norms pass us by. Quick and direct feedback is important in these cases. In this case Israel understood the message and apologized to the teacher. Students are encouraged to follow rules without favoritism of discrimination. If the students see that there is consistency in compliance there will be a change in behavior.

Responsibility is one of the secondary values presented in this case study. Students have a responsibility in doing their homework, instructional activities and working along with their classmates as assigned. They should not be afraid to ask if they have questions and make the teaching and learning process effective. A clear statement regarding what is expected from the student should be stated in the syllabus and it is the student responsibility to follow these institutional rules and policies. When the presentation is uploaded it is saved on the platform.

Whoever notices the wrong identification will have a wrong perception about the students, the course, and the faculty member.

Courage is another of the secondary values presented in this case study. Students must have the courage in their academic life to face their mistakes and consequences since they develop their character strength as they become young professionals. Taking a stand to address wrong-doing and apologizing as Israel did shows courage and hopefully, the commitment of not doing it again. On the other hand, William's lack of integrity shows a character flaw that does not speak well of the type of values that may lead his professional life. They were both irresponsible with their classmates and the teacher, but their reaction in facing the consequences showed different levels of courage.

Question Discussion

1. What actions could the teacher take when realizing the academic misconduct evident in the presentation?
2. What would be the responsibility of the students and faculty in this situation?
3. How can the value of courage be measured?

Conclusion

The quality of being fair, objective, and impartial are essential to perform adequately in different academic environments. Those are the qualities that promote an effective learning process.

Case 9: Procedural Empathy

Joshua Wolf, Elaine Currie, and Jeremy Bourgoin, Vanderbilt University, United States

Synopsis/Summary

Lorraine, a first-year student in the business school at a university in the US is accused of plagiarism on her first paper in a college setting. Lorraine admits to improperly citing her sources and adds that she has never written a research paper before, so she did not know how to create citations. Office staff recognize that Lorraine committed a violation of community standards, but also empathize with Lorraine's lack of understanding about how to cite sources.

Supporting Information

In a meeting with the case investigator, Lorraine explained, "I remembered the professor mentioning to include citations for outside sources, but I wasn't sure what this meant. When I was in high school, we never had to write any papers, so trying to write this one felt overwhelming. I Googled all the information I needed for the paper, and thought it was obvious that it was not my own ideas, but I see now that what the professor meant was for me to include more specifically who wrote the information I included. I really did not mean to cheat; I tried my best to give the professor what she wanted but I didn't know what to do."

Following the meeting, the investigator debriefs Lorraine's statement with another office staff member. The investigator expresses feeling sympathy for Lorraine, as she was not prepared adequately to write the paper, but notes that intent is not a factor in the sanctioning process, and there was clearly plagiarism committed whether Lorraine intended it or not. The investigator feels conflicted about assigning the presumptive sanction to Lorraine for plagiarism when she did not know any better.

Value Discussion

The primary value addressed in this case study is fairness. It is important to recognize that the community standards investigation process can be punitive. As such, reflecting on what specifically your intentions are when assigning sanctions helps ensure that your actions have the desired impact for the students. Furthermore, focusing on educational outcomes ensures fairness in the opportunity for student growth following their interactions with the office. By identifying what additional learning this student could be offered and requiring completion, the student is better positioned to avoid recidivism.

The secondary value addressed in this case study is respect. Respect for students is most apparent when they are given the opportunity to share their specific needs and perspectives throughout the investigative process.

Moving away from punitive measures, or adding more educational measures, in community standards processes allows for more opportunities for conversations with accused students to occur. In this way, students are given more agency in their outcomes and re-education.

Question Discussion

1. How should office staff compartmentalize the student and the student's violation to ensure respect for the student as an individual?
2. How do you ensure the investigative process is educational while still upholding community standards?
3. What are the ethics of demonstrating vulnerability as an office member, and how might this vulnerability increase or decrease the fairness of experiences for accused students?
4. How do you reconcile supporting students through educating them about community standards while simultaneously penalizing them for their previous actions?

Conclusion

The office staff need to reconcile viewing students as their violation versus as individuals to maintain respect for the students and uphold fair procedures.

Case 10: Flagrant Foul on the Faculty

Blaire N. Wilson and Jason T. Ciejka , Emory University, United States

Synopsis/Summary

Dean Shoemake has received complaints from a group of students reported for an academic integrity violation. Their professor accused them of plagiarism on a group assignment. They have heard from other students in the class that the professor handled other plagiarism cases in the class without reporting the students and by allowing them to resubmit their assignment. They are especially concerned that the students who weren't reported are all varsity athletes, and that this special treatment is unfair and inequitable.

Supporting Information

Luke, Nathan, Sarah, and Cara have asked to meet with Dean Shoemake concerning academic misconduct in their class. Luke led the group in explaining that they were reported to the honor code office for plagiarism in their final paper. Luke believed the charge of plagiarism referred to a source that was not cited within the text of the paper but was listed in their bibliography. Luke accepted the blame for this, explaining that his built-in citation tool failed him, and he missed three citations within the text. With this violation, Luke noted, "it would be a miracle for him to pass the class."

Luke learned from his friend Alex, who was assigned to another group, that the professor only gave them a warning when his group missed a few citations in their paper and bibliography and failed to quote and cite some passages that they copied verbatim from sources.

Alex and two of his groupmates are members of the university's basketball team, which is currently number one in conference play and projected to finish the season with strong postseason potential. The other student in the group, Laura, is captain of the volleyball team. She is projected to break the record for "Total Career Aces" early in her senior season.

Luke raised the suspicion of favoritism in his meeting with Dean Shoemake. He pointed to the fact that the other group's alleged plagiarism seems more severe, yet they only received a warning. He argued that this is a clear example of athletes getting special treatment.

Value Discussion

The primary value in this case is fairness. Unless all members of the community are committed to fairness, then the ethics of that community can be called into question. It is commonly said that one negative experience can outweigh the many positives. This is especially true when the negative experience is a case of impartial treatment. How do we restore the faith of a member of our community once they have experienced such treatment? This case study highlights the potential damage when certain groups, like athletes, are perceived as receiving special treatment.

Responsibility, a secondary value, is the expectation of community members to practice the values, standards, and duties set by the community. This may include a duty to report issues of academic misconduct in academic communities. This may include a duty to relinquish some authority as it relates to the grade in the course to an academic integrity process. The responsibility to the community should outweigh one's desire to handle a situation on their own outside the proscribed process.

Question Discussion

1. How should Dean Shoemake respond to the situation?
2. What remedies might Dean Shoemake consider if Luke's complaint is determined to be accurate?
3. If the faculty member is not handling cases in a consistent way that follows university policy, what recourse do the students have?
4. How does the institution balance the need to address the situation with the reported students while also maintaining the privacy and confidentiality of other students in the class?

Conclusion

Centralized academic integrity processes are in place at institutions to help ensure fair and equitable treatment of students across courses; when faculty don't follow these processes, it may undermine equity.

Case 11: Towards Fair and Balanced Budgeting

Greer Murphy, University of Rochester, United States

Synopsis/Summary

After consultation requests and reported cases tripled in five years, Alice (integrity officer at a prestigious, private R1) proposes a budget to invest in (1) education/outreach (helping prevent future infractions) and

(2) adjudication/processing (more efficiently managing reported cases). Administrators allocate 25 percent of her request, enough to cover (1) *or* (2)—not both. Starting incrementally in both areas seems counterproductive but targeting one at the expense of the other seems unfair. For Alice, prioritizing how to spend these funds feels impossible.

Supporting Information

Having a dedicated integrity officer is relatively new for this institution; Alice is the second person to serve in the role. Previously, the integrity system was supported by a faculty director (overseeing adjudication) and hearing board (reviewing evidence, making responsibility decisions, recommending sanctions in cases unresolved through instructor agreement).

In addition to overseeing education/outreach, and confidentially advising students and faculty on fair reporting, Alice's duties entail evaluating the effectiveness of the system and proposing modifications (several of which were recently approved). Alice's job was restructured last year, giving her a direct line to the dean's office and greater access to implement/suggest changes. While the move was positive overall, it came at a cost for Alice (who ended up alienating colleagues and diverting resources from the office where her position was formerly housed).

When Alice and the faculty director propose a budget for additional education/outreach and adjudication/processing to senior administrators, they are pleasantly surprised to see that the response is overwhelmingly positive. Many express broad support: one dean refers to integrity as an "essential" aspect of campus culture, calling the proposal "the most valuable quality assurance investment we could make."

So when Alice follows up, she is particularly shocked to see their budget funded at a fraction of the original request. Asking the deans to reconsider what they allocated might be possible; but given recent structural changes and competing needs in other offices, it seems highly unlikely the budget would be restored to anything near the level Alice and the faculty director expected. Alice fears that pushing too hard might result in receiving an even smaller increase than what is presently allocated (forcing discontinuation of several nascent education/outreach initiatives). Ultimately, Alice realizes she will have to make choices, cut, prioritize. What she doesn't know yet is *how*.

Value Discussion

Fairness is the primary value addressed in this case study. In advocating for a budget proportional to the work she and her staff colleagues are tackling, Alice takes an important step towards ensuring equitable treatment to all within the integrity system. The more resources dedicated to outreach/educating students about integrity, the fairer it is to hold them accountable for not practicing it. But upholding integrity is a collaborative, system-wide endeavor—education/outreach takes work—and must be resourced accordingly. If that is unfeasible, it is only fair to adjust expectations of what staff in an integrity office like Alice's can accomplish.

Respect is the secondary value addressed in this case study. Much of what integrity officers do depends on soft influence: persuasion, reputation, giving and receiving respect. Alice may not be able to change her budget situation. But she can exhibit professionalism and seriousness, making the case for why funds are needed and establishing herself as credible and worthy of respect. To instantiate the collegiality and collaboration that creates respect, Alice should also show she knows her priorities are not the only ones that count. She can, by communicating clearly what programs she may have to discontinue, acknowledging the position deans are in, and accepting she might not get her way.

Question Discussion

1. Is this decision really the end of the budget road for Alice? Does she have to accept a budget she is concerned might not be fair? What other choice(s) might she have?
2. What considerations guide or should guide Alice's choice to allocate funding to education/outreach or adjudication/processing? When there's not enough to go around, what does fair budgeting look like?
3. Once decisions are made, what considerations guide how Alice delivers the news back to stakeholders on campus? In this context, what does fair, respectful communication look like?

Conclusion

While holding students accountable, integrity officers and administrators should support the personal, institutional practice of fairness and respect, and should understand budgeting as an integral expression of that effort.

Case 12: Socialize with Specialists to Spot and Stem Spinning

Abby Pfeiffer, Heather Frase, Katie Frank, Ben McDermott, and Kacy Vargas, Western Governors University, United States

Synopsis/Summary

Scott evaluates written work submitted by students in history courses, and he is concerned about the possibility that a student is "spinning" their work. Scott contacts the academic authenticity team to evaluate the submission. Ben, one of the advisors, reviews the student submission. The cross-department collaboration begins at this stage, as Scott and Ben work together to determine if this is an authenticity or a writing issue, in order to customize student support.

Supporting Information

Spinning is defined as "a technique to generate seemingly original content from old content by replacing words or phrases with synonyms" (Bailey, 2018). Scott knows collaboration is crucial to student fairness, as the academic authenticity team has educated faculty members about the potential for spinning versus writing issues. As Scott often works with the authenticity team, he requests Ben's academic authenticity expertise to identify unfamiliar wording and potential location of the original source.

As Scott is aware of what spinning is, after he completes the referral to the authenticity team, he emails Ben to indicate which specific phrases he found problematic as a subject matter expert (SME). For example, he noted that the student called the Great Depression a "tremendous melancholy," which is not a common or standard phrase to refer to that historical event. Additionally, Scott also noted specific phrases that were incomprehensible, which was another clue to Scott that the student may have spun their work. Scott noted in his email that the information appeared to have come from the course resource, which can help the authenticity team focus their investigation.

Ben receives Scott's email and uses the information provided by Scott to begin investigating the student submission. Ben follows a standard authenticity review process, which is applied to every student concerned for fairness and to determine if it's a spinning concern or a writing concern. If the student's submission is determined to be a writing concern, they will be routed to the appropriate support team. In this instance, after Ben finishes his investigation, he was able to successfully find the original source that the student spun, leading to a warning sent to the student. The combination of the resource identification and the authenticity review process led to a conclusive academic authenticity violation for the student.

Value Discussion

This case study is related to the primary fundamental value of fairness. As academic authenticity advisors are not SMEs in the content of student work, they cannot be expected to know what specific irregularities to look for in suspected spun work. They coordinate with faculty, who serve as SMEs, to identify any area of the student submission that is problematic. This approach is fair for students as their work is reviewed by a trained academic authenticity advisor who follows a consistent review process. Coupled with assistance from the content SMEs, this provides an equitable, objective review of the student work.

This case study is related to the secondary fundamental value of responsibility. Students are responsible for submitting original work, and they are required to acknowledge our academic authenticity policies prior to submission. The responsibility of the faculty is to provide academic support for students, review work in a non-biased manner, and provide resources and support for authenticity related concerns. The academic authenticity team, along with all university staff and faculty, are responsible for upholding the value and integrity of the university's degrees. By working together, faculty and authenticity team members identify instances where student work is and is not authentic. Additionally, this value is also displayed during crucial conversations with students about the importance of original work and academic integrity, and the importance of accountability with institutional rules and policies.

Question Discussion

1. How is spinning different from other forms of academic dishonesty?
2. How does spinning impact fairness for students in higher education?
3. How can SMEs work together to assist students with their academic responsibility to create original work?

Conclusion

Spinning creates inequity by allowing students that spin their work to gain a degree without demonstrating mastery, which is inherently unfair, and it's the students' responsibility to submit original work.

Reference

Bailey, J. "A brief history of article spinning." *Plagiarism Today*, 2018, March 8. https://www.plagiarismtoday.com/2018/03/08/a-brief-history-of-article-spinning/.

Chapter 4
Respect

Chapter Contents:

Respect and Honor Through Intentional Proactive Student Actions
  Sally Sledge, Norfolk State University, United States
  Pam Pringle, Christopher Newport University (retired), United States
The Emotional Rollercoaster of Reporting
  Laura Facciolo, McMaster University, Canada
  Elyse Redquest, Enrique Ponce, Iryna Pavlova, and Danielle Palombi, Sheridan
  College, Canada
Time Is a Non-Renewable Resource
  Blaire N. Wilson and Jason T. Ciejka, Emory University, United States
Email Déjà Vu
  Jason T. Ciejka and Blaire N. Wilson, Emory University, United States
When the Bones Are Good: Laying the Foundation for Faculty
  Elaine Currie, Joshua Wolf, and Jeremy Bourgoin, Vanderbilt University, United
  States
Punishment and Rehabilitation
  Pamela Kennedy and Hans Kunov, University of Toronto, Canada
Tipping the Scale: Mental Health and Outcomes
  Elaine Currie, Joshua Wolf and Jeremy Bourgoin, Vanderbilt University, United
  States
Personalized and Supportive Proctoring Processes
  Carissa Pittsenberger, Western Governors University, United States
  Maureen O'Brien, Western Governors University (retired), United States
Advising Not Policing: Respecting the Students
  Joshua Wolf, Elaine Currie, and Jeremy Bourgoin, Vanderbilt University, United
  States

Respect in academic communities is reciprocal and requires showing respect for oneself as well. Examples of respect include receiving feedback willingly, practicing active listening, showing empathy, seeking open communication, affirming others, and recognizing the consequences of our word and actions on others. It is not just that it is expecting trust from others but you also want to make sure that it is respectful, which shows that this trust goes both ways. To be clear, this is not only between individuals or between an individual and an institution, but one's self as well—respecting oneself. This can of course be completed in many different ways. As educators, we want students to have an active role in contributing to discussion and it means at times there are going to be some discussions where not everybody is going to agree. Faculty need to recognize students as individuals and to take seriously the ideas that those students have, respectfully. Respect is also having the faculty give full honest feedback and actionable feedback. Within respect in the institution, we must embrace that it is healthy to have some spirited discussions. The respect shown among the discussions gives the ability for individuals to have those disagreements but also to be able to proceed forward and to express their views.

There are nine case studies in this book which address the primary value of respect

Case Study Focused on the Student. There is one case study which primarily addresses the student perspective. In "Case 1: *Respect and Honor Through Intentional Proactive Student Actions*" two students were invited to join the newly formed honor council. They expand their breadth of experience by working with other members to develop activities that could be used to encourage ethical behavior.

Case Studies Focused on the Faculty. There are four case studies which primarily address this perspective.

In "Case 2: *The Emotional Rollercoaster of Reporting*" an international student received a suspected breach notification and contacts her professor about her personal situation: she is financially unstable, has been avoiding communication with her professor due to language barriers, and is generally feeling overwhelmed.

In "Case 3: *Time Is a Non-Renewable Resource*" a professor designed a study evaluating her department's new curriculum and plans on publishing the results . . . She discovers a blatant case of group collaboration on an exam that was expected to be completed individually and the cheating has potentially compromised the findings of the study.

In "Case 4: *Email Déjà Vu*" a faculty chair sent a thoughtful message to the working group members thanking them for their contributions at the conclusion of the project. The following semester, she received a thank you email from an administrator overseeing another committee she served on, and the message was clearly plagiarized.

In "Case 5: *When the Bones Are Good: Laying the Foundation for Faculty*" a professor submits multiple reports of alleged academic integrity violations to the Office of Community Standards. When he meets with a staff member to discuss these violations, he is unprepared, and this significantly slows the investigative process.

Case Studies Focused on the Academic Integrity Office and Office of Community Standards.

There are four case studies which primarily address this perspective. Two of the cases address student strife after the fact. In "Case 6: *Punishment and Rehabilitation*" a remorseful student meets to discuss his offense of unauthorized assistance. In "Case 7: *Tipping the Scale: Mental Health and Outcomes*" a student is reported to the Office of Community Standards for Googling a final exam question. Based on mitigated circumstances, the office staff are conflicted about whether to give them the standard penalty or preserve the student's mental health.

In "Case 8: *Personalized and Supportive Proctoring Processes*" a student is enrolled in a competency-based program requiring a significant number of online-proctored assessments. The technology demands, and unknown, remote proctor exacerbated her test anxiety. Her faculty mentor needed to find an option that would allow her to be successful while maintaining standards and academic integrity.

The final case focuses on the academic integrity office addressing unconscious bias. In "Case 9: *Advising Not Policing: Respecting the Students*" a staff member felt the evidence pointed to the student being guilty of the violation prior to the meeting. The staff framed her questions in a way that leads the student to feel criminalized demonstrating unconscious bias.

In addition to the nine case studies in this chapter on respect, twelve other case studies in this book address respect as a secondary value. Refer to that value chapter as shown for an introduction to each case study.

Honesty:

- *Photoshop: The Easiest (Worst!) Way Out*

Trust:

- *Where in the Metaverse Is Boris' Voice?*
- *My Students, My Research Subjects—Trust in Faculty, Researcher, and Student Relationships*
- *But They'll Never Know*
- *Using Relational Coordination to Promote Academic Integrity*
- *Capturing the Impostor Syndrome Through Turnitin*

Fairness:

- *Can't Put My Finger on It*
- *Towards Fair and Balanced Budgeting*
- *Procedural Empathy*

Responsibility:

- *Scaffolding Writing for an A*
- *Abuse of Power by Medical Teachers: Can We Still Become Role Models?*

Courage:

- *But I Know This Student Well*

Case 1: Respect and Honor Through Intentional Proactive Student Actions

Sally Sledge, Norfolk State University, United States
Pam Pringle, Christopher Newport University (retired), United States

Synopsis/Summary

Ashton and Blake, juniors majoring in business, were invited to join the newly formed honor council at CBC University. Both are in the top 10 percent of their class. They accept. They meet in the library with the other members to develop a list of classroom and campus activities that could be used to encourage ethical behavior on campus and promote the values of respect and honesty within the student body and the campus community.

Supporting Information

Each department at CBCU was asked to identify 1 (or 2) student(s) to become officers of the new university student honor council. Selected students must meet the provided criteria (3.0 GPA, good academic standing, personal statement re council involvement, and faculty recommendation). The business school faculty chose Ashton and Blake. They more than meet the requirements for selection. Both have had experience with situations involving academic integrity and have dealt with them in an exemplary manner.

Ashton's roommate was charged with plagiarism several months ago, and initially denied it. While tidying up their room a few days later, Ashton picked up some paper from the floor that clearly showed his roommate had indeed plagiarized. Ashton showed the roommate the papers and encouraged them to admit it and acknowledge it was wrong. Ashton offered to go to the professor with them for moral support. The roommate did go to the professor with Ashton, confessed, acknowledging Ashton's role in helping them to realize the negative impact of their action. Separately, Blake had been offered a copy of an upcoming test in a marketing class. Blake refused it but after some thought went to the professor to alert them to the situation.

"I am excited about this opportunity," said Blake. Ashton responded, "Yes, I am too. I think there are things that we could do to develop a culture of respect and honor here at CBCU." Blake nodded. "Let's send an email to the other members to meet together and brainstorm ideas."

Over the next few months, the students used several methods to get data on their fellow students' perceptions about honor and integrity at CBCU. They used focus groups, talking informally with their dorm mates and classmates, as well as fraternity brothers and sisters. They used Survey Monkey to ask faculty their thoughts. They talked to friends at other colleges to get their input. They also researched university honor codes and university honor councils online. They learned a lot about their peers during this process. Two themes kept recurring in the feedback they received. The first theme was that students wanted to feel respected throughout any interaction with an honor council or honor code. The second theme was that students wanted to have honest conversations and communication with administrators, faculty, and staff.

Value Discussion

The primary value addressed in this case study is respect. Ashton shows respect for both his roommate and the professor and helps the roommate recognize the harm caused by their actions. Blake likewise shows respect to the professor whose test has been compromised as well as to the other students in the class. Seeking input from others when identifying possible integrity activities shows respect to all who will be affected by the changes in campus culture. Exhibiting respect can be achieved by recognizing each individual's boundaries, traditions, privacy, confidentiality, personal space, limitations, previous experiences, and other sensitive information.

Honesty includes doing one's own work, taking responsibility for one's own actions, appropriately citing sources, telling the truth, and fostering an attitude of objectivity. The case discussion questions encourage students to address why it is important to remain truthful and objective with others and oneself. When an individual does their own work honestly, they are respecting themselves and those around them. Students' mindsets can be positively impacted by traditions such as regular honor committee meetings and focus groups to discuss these topics. Actively participating in a culture that values honesty will have a significant impact on both their professional and personal future lives.

Question Discussion

1. How can students promote respect and honesty on their campuses to reinforce a culture of academic integrity?
2. How can administrators and faculty support students in promoting these values?
3. How else can we promote honor and respect in our campus/school community?
4. Why is all this important? What is the impact of post-graduation?

Conclusion

This case demonstrates how college students can initiate ethics-based activities that engage many campus community members and promote honor, respect, academic integrity, and in time, positively impact campus culture.

Case 2: The Emotional Rollercoaster of Reporting

Laura Facciolo, McMaster University, Canada
Elyse Redquest, Enrique Ponce, Iryna Pavlova, and Danielle Palombi, Sheridan College, Canada

Synopsis/Summary

Karolina is a second-year international student at an accredited college in Canada. After receiving a suspected breach notification, Karolina realizes that the potential sanctions against her work for suspected plagiarism will significantly affect her grade in the course. Karolina contacts her professor and describes her personal situation: she is financially unstable, has been avoiding communication with her professor due to language barriers, and is generally feeling overwhelmed. The professor contacts the academic integrity office for guidance.

Supporting Information

After receiving a worried email from her student, Prof. Rodriquez began feeling quite uneasy with her decision to investigate Karolina for suspected plagiarism. While waiting for the academic integrity office to respond to her inquiry, she had started questioning her instructional practices and pedagogical decisions. She knew that Karolina struggled with English language proficiency, but she thought that she had cultivated an equitable classroom environment that prioritized inclusivity and respect. She asked herself, "Did I do enough to support Karolina's academic success?" She had not expected Karolina to say that language barriers had prevented her from seeking help with her coursework. She was experiencing a range of emotions, from guilt to anxiety. She felt that perhaps she had acted on impulse in filing a suspected breach report and had not fully considered her student's personal context.

Later that day, the academic integrity office contacted Dr. Rodriquez to further discuss the suspected breach. During their meeting,

Dr. Rodriquez explained her feelings: "I don't know if I should have reported Karolina for suspected plagiarism. She struggles with oral and written English language proficiency, and I'm feeling like I'm failing my student by having filed an investigation report." The academic integrity office manager chimed in, "It is normal to be experiencing a spectrum of emotions during an academic integrity investigation, since teaching often requires emotional and personal investment." This resonated with Dr. Rodriquez: she was very passionate about her course and worked hard to create connections with her students. The manager continued, "Let's think about how formally reporting a suspected academic integrity breach can actually introduce students to academic resources that can support their success."

Value Discussion

The primary value in this case is respect. Given that teaching is a caring profession, approaching academic integrity unemotionally may prove impossible. In this case study, the academic integrity office acknowledged that emotions are inherent to academic integrity investigations but encouraged a mindset shift by asking the instructor to consider how upholding the values of academic integrity through reporting is an act of pedagogical care and respect for oneself, for the intellectual contributions of other scholars, and for their students. Faculty members demonstrate respect for teaching and learning by providing students with the opportunity to reflect on and learn from their mistakes to develop as scholarly individuals.

A secondary value found in this case is fairness. Although formally reporting a suspected academic integrity breach can be an emotional experience, consistently upholding institutional academic integrity policies and procedures is a demonstration of fairness. In this case study, Dr. Rodriquez was concerned that her decision to formally report Karolina was unfair, given that Karolina expressed that language barriers impeded her ability to seek academic support. As the academic integrity office affirmed, though, taking academic integrity investigations seriously can enable reflective pedagogical practices that respond to individual student needs, as well as foster educational equity by introducing students to resources (e.g., tutoring) that can support their academic success.

Question Discussion

1. What role does the academic integrity office play in providing support to faculty members?
2. As an impartial resource, how can the academic integrity office demonstrate compassion and empathy for faculty members?
3. How can faculty members break the stigma surrounding academic misconduct?

Conclusion

Since teaching can be emotionally laborious, it is important that reporting is framed as practice of pedagogical care and respect—for oneself, one's students, and the scholarly community.

References

Biswas, A. E. (2015). "I second that emotion: Minding how plagiarism feels. Teaching/Writing: The Journal of Writing," *Teacher Education* 4, no. 1 (2015). https://scholarworks.wmich.edu/wte/vol4/iss1/7

Robinson, R., and Openo, J. (2021). "The emotional labour of academic integrity: How does it feel?," *Canadian Perspectives on Academic Integrity* 4, no. 1 (2021). https://doi.org/10.11575/cpai.v4i1.71350

Case 3: Time Is a Non-Renewable Resource

Blaire N. Wilson and Jason T. Ciejka, Emory University, United States

Synopsis/Summary

Professor Jones has designed a four-year study evaluating her department's new curriculum. She intends on publishing her findings and has shared this with her students each semester. In year 3 of the study, she discovers a blatant case of group collaboration on an exam that was expected to be completed individually. The cheating has potentially compromised the findings of the study. Professor Jones is reluctant to report this to the academic integrity office but is also angered by this discovery.

Supporting Information

Professor Jones is reviewing educational data related to her course, which typically sees an enrollment of 150 students across multiple sections each semester. The alleged academic misconduct involves 15 students in the course, amounting to 10 percent of the course enrollment.

This course is a prerequisite for a popular major at the institution and is commonly considered a gateway course. Students who fail or withdraw from this course in their second year often change their summer plans and enroll in a summer section so as not to disrupt their course plans and planned schedule for their third year.

Course evaluations commonly describe the course as "difficult" and "time-intensive." The course evaluations submitted by students generally insinuate that the course is too rigorous and the content too ambitious.

The students who allegedly cheated communicated in a group chat, which was shared with the professor after the exam by a student invited to the chat. The participants in the chat discussed meeting together for the exam and settled on a location and time. The professor found similar answers across the exam and noted some students completed the exam at an alarmingly fast pace. The university has the ability to collect additional evidence in the form of student locations based on card access to buildings and Wi-Fi access points.

Value Discussion

The primary value in this case is respect. Recognizing the potential consequences our actions have on others is a key element in demonstrating respect. Professor Jones made a point to share that her course is contributing to a research project. By engaging in academic misconduct, these students have prioritized their grade over their respect for their instructor and her research. Professor Jones has an opportunity to show respect to the rest of the students enrolled in the course in how she chooses to respond.

One secondary value seen in this case is responsibility. Professor Jones has a responsibility to report this information to the proper channels at her institution, despite what it may cost her. Professor Jones is expected to model good behavior for her students and that includes reporting this violation, a circumstance that may impact her larger research study. Similarly, the students were expected and had a responsibility to follow the same set of guidelines and instructions for the exam as their peers.

Another secondary value in this case is honesty. This case touches on the idea of honesty in that Professor Jones is contemplating turning a blind eye to the issue. On the one hand, reporting the case may cause complications when she is ready to punish the student. On the other hand, failing to report the incident and obscuring how it has potentially compromised her data would be an ethical breach and an instance of research misconduct in and of itself. Honest reporting of data is paramount to the integrity of research; without it the trust in the validity of the research erodes away.

Question Discussion

1. How can Professor Jones overcome her reluctance to report?
2. Would engaging students in conversation about the significance of this class and the research study decrease the likelihood of cheating?
3. Is it appropriate for Professor Jones to advocate for a harsher set of consequences in the academic integrity process because of her personal stake in the research project?
4. How has the design of this course increased its susceptibility to instances of academic dishonesty?
5. How can the academic integrity administrator help restore respect between the students and Professor Jones in this situation?

Conclusion

Respect requires mutual understanding and regard for the goals and values of others; academic integrity can break down when individuals lose sight of the need for respect.

Case 4: Email Déjà Vu

Jason T. Ciejka and Blaire N. Wilson, Emory University, United States

Synopsis/Summary

The faculty chair of a working group, Professor Silva, sent a long and thoughtful message to the working group members thanking them for their contributions at the conclusion of the project. The following semester, Professor Silva received a thank you email from an administrator overseeing another committee she served on. The message was clearly plagiarized from Professor Silva's note to the working group.

Supporting Information

Professor Silva chaired a faculty working group on inclusive pedagogy that culminated in a curated list of resources and training for the faculty and a proposal to hire new staff dedicated to inclusive pedagogy in the university's center for teaching. Professor Silva was proud of the committee's work and sent a detailed message thanking the group for their work. The note lauded the group's "bold decision-making and visionary approach to inclusive pedagogy."

The following semester, Professor Silva worked on a faculty committee charged with recommending changes to the faculty hiring process. She was surprised to see a very similar thank you note from an administrator who served in an *ex officio* capacity on the inclusive pedagogy working group. Although the original thank you note was quite specific to the inclusive pedagogy project, the plagiarized email just swapped out some details, praising the "bold decision-making and visionary approach to faculty hiring" among other heavily plagiarized passages. As a result, the message rang hollow.

Not only was Professor Silva disappointed by the plagiarism, but she also felt that the stock response to the committee's work undercut the real value of the project.

Value Discussion

The primary value in this case is respect. The administrator's decision to plagiarize could demonstrate a lack of respect for faculty colleagues and the work of the committee. The administrator may not have considered the consequences of plagiarizing a thank you note, including the potential to damage their relationship with faculty and their credibility. How the situation is handled, especially if there is open communication and dialogue between the faculty and the administrator, might help to restore the value of respect in this situation.

A secondary value shown in this case is responsibility. At many institutions, the plagiarism of an administrative message might not violate any university policies, but that does not make this situation less troubling. Faculty and administrators alike have a responsibility to model good behavior, including writing communications that follow the standards of academic integrity.

The final value portrayed in this case is honesty. The administrator compromised the value of honesty by making the decision to take a short-cut and plagiarize a note from a colleague rather than taking the time to write a personal message. Not only does the plagiarized communication fail to give credit to the author, but it is also seemingly disingenuous in its praise of the faculty committee.

Question Discussion

1. Is plagiarizing an administrative message as significant as plagiarizing an academic assignment?
2. Should the faculty say something to the administrator about the plagiarism?
3. What potential power dynamics might impact how the faculty responds to the situation?
4. How does this situation undermine the respect between the two parties and the work of the committees?

Conclusion

Faculty and administrators have a duty to model academic integrity and respect the work of their colleagues even in instances where the stakes might seem low.

Case 5: When the Bones Are Good: Laying the Foundation for Faculty

Elaine Currie, Joshua Wolf, and Jeremy Bourgoin, Vanderbilt University, United States

Synopsis/Summary

A professor at a university in the US submits multiple reports of alleged academic integrity violations to the Office of Community

Standards where he works. He meets with a staff member to discuss these violations but arrives at the meeting unprepared and significantly slows the investigative process.

Supporting Information

Faculty members who submit reports of alleged academic integrity violations in their classes are contacted by an investigator from the Office of Community Standards to set up a meeting in which to discuss the allegations in more detail. In their initial contact, the investigator provides a list of recommended documentation for faculty to collect and bring to their scheduled meeting.

Dr. Lewis is a professor in the College of Communications at a university in the US. After submitting multiple reports of alleged academic integrity violations to the Office of Community Standards, he meets with Beth, an office staff member, to discuss his allegations. Dr. Lewis is unprepared and does not bring documentation to support his allegations. Because of this, Beth must follow up via email to request the missing documents. Dr. Lewis takes two weeks to respond, slowing the process.

At their meeting, Beth requests that Dr. Lewis provide the documentation listed in her email, to which he responds that he still needs to compile it. When Beth follows up with Dr. Lewis after the meeting, she receives no response. Beth is unable to meet with the accused students until she receives the materials from Dr. Lewis. As a result, students are left waiting to meet with Beth for months.

Value Discussion

The primary value addressed in this case study is respect. As such, it highlights the ways in which the academic integrity process is shaped by the role that reporting faculty play in the efficiency and effectiveness of community standards investigations. It points to the importance of respect for the investigation process by reporters, as full participation and preparation for involvement is necessary to move through the investigation efficiently and effectively. Abusing the process demonstrates a lack of respect for the accused students, who are forced to wait until the reporter has participated to share their side of the story.

This case study highlights the responsibility, as a secondary value, that faculty members have to be active participants in the processes associated with the community standards office. Central to this are expectation setting and a faculty reporting culture driven by upper-level administration and department heads. All parties have a responsibility to take a unified stance on the importance of fully participating in the reporting process to create an environment where the Office of Community Standards can be successful. Additionally, this case highlights the responsibility of staff members to set expectations for faculty participation, and to guide them through the process successfully.

This case study also highlights trust as a secondary value. In the context of investigations regarding students' academic integrity, trust is necessary for the success of the case. Without trust, the relationship between office staff and reporting faculty members is tense, which can slow down a case and negatively impact the accused students' experience. Building trust between office staff and faculty relies on each side doing their share of the work to ensure that investigations are conducted thoroughly and efficiently before delivering student outcomes. This case highlights the proceedings of an academic integrity case where trust has been broken between the investigator and the reporting faculty member.

Question Discussion

1. How do offices standardize reporting and information gathering procedures to ensure each accused student is provided a fair and consistent investigation?
2. How do office staff cultivate an open line of communication with faculty about the responsibilities associated with reporting alleged academic integrity violations?
3. How do office staff ensure that faculty are aware of their processes and the level of participation needed for those processes?

Conclusion

Office staff and campus partners need to reestablish roles and expectations around faculty respect and responsibility in the integrity process, so as to respect students' and staff members' time.

Case 6: Punishment and Rehabilitation

Pamela Kennedy and Hans Kunov, University of Toronto, Canada

Synopsis/Summary

A remorseful student meets to discuss his offense of unauthorized assistance. Although the work in the integrity office is to uphold the university's high standards, it is also a part of the educational process. Everybody makes mistakes; some more egregious, and some more deliberate than others. Should the focus be on the transgression? Or should the focus be on educating and restoring self-esteem and confidence? Does the focus change when meeting with repeat offenders or offenders who initially lie?

Supporting Information

It can be taken for granted that everyone is exposed to temptations and that sometimes we give in to them. Our personal moral compass and the code of ethics that apply in a specific field should stop us, but experience shows us that we occasionally fail. Some students may think of academic offenses as a game to be won, lying rather than owning up to their transgression, but a much larger group feels badly about committing one.

The student in this case study enters the meeting, visibly upset. After outlining some procedures, the AI officer asks the student for a response to the allegation.

The student says, "It's true. I'm guilty. I apologize to you and my instructor. I'm ashamed and will never do this again."

The AI officer applauds the student for taking ownership for his mistake: "I appreciate you coming clean right away. I have great respect for that. Although you did offend, the fact that you are taking accountability for your actions speaks well of your character. We are all human and we all make mistakes. I will have to sanction you, and you won't like it, but you will move on from this. Don't ever let me see you in this office again. Put this behind you, but never forget it."

The student appears relieved and expresses gratitude for the valuable words. He shares how he will behave differently in the future: "Thank you. Next time I will make sure I reach out to my instructor if I'm struggling."

The AI officer further educates: "Yes, please do. Instructors, TAs, and your academic advisor are all available to help. There are so many resources at the university to assist you. Reach out. You're a good student. I wish you all the best in your academic career and beyond."

Value Discussion

The primary value discussed in this case study is respect. It illustrates a situation where a student, despite violating the rules, is given encouragement and respect. The AI officer did not shame the distressed student, but rather tried to lift the student up; focused on the student's impressive and appropriate response to the allegation. He also discussed various resources to utilize in the future. Should respect be reciprocal? For example, if a student displays a lack of respect during the meeting (lying, defiant), should the AI officer change his approach to a focus on the transgression?

This case study also illustrates the importance of honesty. The AI officer stated "we are all human." By doing this, he is in a sense leveling with a student and showing honesty about our own fallible nature. This can reduce excessive shame the student may feel and allow him/her to move on from the situation. The case study also shows how maintaining fairness can, at times, seem harsh; the student must be sanctioned regardless of his respectful approach to the meeting. The AI officer encouraged the student to learn from his mistake and move on.

Question Discussion

1. Most meetings in the AI office are brief. When presented with the evidence (and mostly by simply saying that it exists), about 80 percent of students admit to the transgression. Another 15 percent admit reluctantly or after seeing the evidence. This leaves five to ten or more minutes of the allotted time. Is it appropriate and effective to end meetings with encouragement? Or, should AI meetings stay focused on the transgression?
2. Acknowledging that the grapevine will inform most of the student body about decisions and actions in the integrity office, does the rehabilitative component of the meeting serve a positive purpose?

3. Will a rehabilitative component be seen as a prosecutorial weakness to be exploited? Some students may think they can get a more lenient sanction if they lay out a plan for a clean life. Does it encourage "cheating as a game to be won"?

4. The meeting in the integrity office is always stressful, and sometimes quite emotional for the student. In addition, some feel very vulnerable. They will probably never forget the experience. Is the AI office the right place for soothing talk, or should that be left with professional advisors at the departmental or faculty level?

5. Family members, in particular parents, are typically deeply concerned about the consequences of academic misconduct. When present at meetings they will sometimes defend the student's behavior, but they will invariably talk about their son's or daughter's good character. In what way, and how far should the AI office play along with the student's relative?

6. Wherever students go after graduation, and especially in the professions, there will be codes of ethics. Putting the academic transgression in that perspective will illustrate the importance of integrity. Is this an opportunity or is it an inappropriate extrapolation of the issue at hand?

Conclusion

Respect, and fairness, are values in the AI office as they are in student behavior. We postulate that it means an attempt at rehabilitation as well as punishment for transgressions.

Case 7: Tipping the Scale: Mental Health and Outcomes

Elaine Currie, Joshua Wolf, and Jeremy Bourgoin, Vanderbilt University, United States

Synopsis/Summary

Trish, a second-year student in the School of Engineering at a university in the US, is reported to the Office of Community Standards for Googling a final exam question. The student expresses distress as a result of the investigation, and personal and family issues that impacted their decision to cheat. Office staff are conflicted about whether to give them the standard penalty for their actions, or to deliver an individualized outcome for the preservation of the student's mental health.

Supporting Information

In a meeting with a staff member from the Office of Community Standards Trish said, "I did Google question 3C during my final exam, but I did not Google any other questions. I studied as hard as I could for this final, but it still wasn't enough and when I got to question 3C I panicked and Googled it without thinking. I have never done anything like this before, but my dad has been in the hospital for the last two weeks and I've been having extreme anxiety about his status. My dad pays for my college, and I really just want to make him proud by performing well in school, so when I got to question 3C on the exam and didn't know the answer I looked for it online without even thinking. The last thing I need is to fail this class because of one stupid mistake. I just want to be able to spend time with my dad and focus on him healing, not retaking this class. I know I messed up and I feel terrible for violating community standards, but it was just one mistake." The staff member knows that the penalty for Googling a question during an exam is typically failure in the course but worries that if Trish were to fail her mental health would take a rapid decline due to the link between her dad and her education.

Value Discussion

This case study investigates the concept of respect, as the primary value, by demonstrating how staff members can show empathy to students despite procedural requirements. The dimensions here include external factors contributing to student mental health concerns, which can be in conflict with the scripted procedures of the conduct process. The issue of respect concerns the accused student holistically, accounting for factors that may be tangentially relevant to the violation in question, and how those factors should be considered. Factors used to decide when to amend student sanctions in the conduct process should consider respect for the student.

Fairness is addressed in this case study, as a secondary value, as it explores the possibility of flexible sanctioning so as to consider each accused student equitably. Many of the students that meet with the Office of Community Standards are experiencing distress of some kind, but it is important to reflect on when it is fair to provide individualized outcomes and when it is fairer to follow outlined policies and procedures.

Question Discussion

1. As a staff member, what responsibility do we have to preserve student mental health as a display of respect to the student when it conflicts with upholding community standards?
2. How do we better prepare office staff for cases involving critical mental health crises?
3. How (and should) office staff modify outcomes in cases to help students experience less distress while still promoting fairness throughout the process?

Conclusion

Respect is a critical component of amending office procedure in an effort to be fair across student needs while also maintaining the integrity of the process.

Case 8: Personalized and Supportive Proctoring Processes

Carissa Pittsenberger, Western Governors University, United States
Maureen O'Brien, Western Governors University (retired), United States

Synopsis/Summary

Sade Student is enrolled in a competency-based program requiring a significant number of online-proctored assessments. She attempted one assessment using the standard process, but the technology demands, and unknown, remote proctor exacerbated her test anxiety. Sade wanted to unenroll, convinced that there would not be a pathway for successful completion of the program. Sade's faculty mentor needed to find an option that would allow Sade to be successful while maintaining standards and academic integrity.

Supporting Information

Sade Student was excited to register for her competency-based degree program and understood some assessments would have remote proctoring. She had a chance to take a practice test but realizing someone would be looking at her home through a remote camera and scanning her room made her very nervous. As Sade had career goals that were dependent upon completing a degree in her field, she worked through the course material until she felt ready to verify her competency.

Sade continued to have some reservations about the proctored assessment experience, but she was confident in her skills and decided to move forward. Sade took her first assessment, but her concerns about the proctor kept swirling around in her head. She found it hard to concentrate and didn't do well on her assessment. She was so uncomfortable, she decided she couldn't continue in the program and told her faculty mentor that she was going to drop out.

Manuel Mentor is trained on how to ask probing questions when students are struggling. After some discussion, Sade shared she had been a victim of a home invasion and found the presence of an unknown remote proctor looking at her home very disturbing. She knew the content and was disappointed that the situation did not allow her to show her competency and how this might impact her educational goals. Manuel and Sade meet with the integrity office and the Student Success Team who discuss options for Sade. Sade considers if the options meet her needs as she decides whether to continue with her program.

Value Discussion

Respect is the primary value addressed in this case study. Respecting our students includes understanding their life experiences. This may create an emotional reaction to situations that we do not understand unless we take the time to listen. An initial reaction may be to tell Sade that she knew she would need to take remotely proctored assessments. That approach would have caused Sade to drop out of her program. Balancing the needs of the student with the expectations requires a respectful and open level of communication supported with social emotional learning.

The outcome of the situation may be significantly changed depending upon how a mentor and student communicate.

Fairness, as a second value addressed in the case study, might dictate equal treatment of all students, requiring all to have the exact same proctoring experience. That inflexible approach would have resulted in a student dropping out. Another extreme would be to waive the need for proctoring assessments, however, that approach would not be fair to other students. Test security and verifying the authenticity of the student's work ensures the value of all student degrees. Fair and equal are not the same thing. A personalized approach that maintains the high level of integrity provides a fair and secure option.

Another secondary value addressed in this case study is trust. Building an atmosphere of trust requires participation from all involved. Developing a system around supporting students in a way that allows the student to trust that the staff of the university and any partners are working to provide the best experience and learning environment possible is important. For students to communicate honestly about needs and expectations, they need to trust and feel safe in doing so. In addition, building relationships with individual students provides connection and trust from the faculty and staff side. Coming together with trust can lead to more collaboration for better results.

Question Discussion

1. What options should be provided to balance the need for test security and an understanding approach to each student's experience in the proctoring process?
2. How is a personalized learning journey used to support academic integrity and individual student needs? What are the benefits and risks in providing an accommodation?
3. What can be done to create an environment where students feel comfortable asking for help instead of dropping out?

Conclusion

Faculty must respect student needs for accommodations and respect and fairness when they are warranted so academic integrity guardrails do not create barriers to student success for specific individual learners.

Case 9: Advising Not Policing: Respecting the Students

Joshua Wolf, Elaine Currie, and Jeremy Bourgoin, Vanderbilt University, United States

Synopsis/Summary

Rebecca is a white, cisgender female staff member in the Office of Community Standards at a predominantly white institution in the US. She is assigned a case investigating a black male student accused of falsifying lab data. Prior to meeting with the student, Rebecca felt the evidence pointed to the student being guilty of the violation. Because of this, Rebecca enters the investigation with unconscious bias and frames her questions in a way that leads the student to feel criminalized.

Supporting Information

Students accused of violating community standards at the university take part in an investigative process which begins with a meeting with Rebecca, the investigator. Rebecca's role is to collect the student's statement and any additional documentation about the events in question. In this role, Rebecca is meant to be a neutral participant in the process and has no say in any outcomes or sanctions that the student receives. Following the meeting, Rebecca's written report of what the student shared with her will serve as the student's official statement for the investigation. Rebecca's questions are meant to guide her in writing this report and are meant to convey the student's perspective of the violation in question. During her investigation with the student, Rebecca asks questions such as:

"Why did you falsify lab data?"
"Did you falsify data because you felt unprepared?"
"I assume your high school didn't prepare you for rigorous coursework, is that why you cheated?"

Value Discussion

Respect for students in the investigative process occurs when students are given a fair, unbiased, opportunity to share their experience of situations in question. This case study relates to the ways in which accountability processes can lead to biases and assumptions that can color office procedure and student outcomes, and how these assumptions diminish the agency and personhood of involved students.

The fairness of all cases moving through the investigative process is violated when assumptions are made about individual students and case facts. Fair investigation relies on case facts and individual accounts of the events in question, from both the accuser and the accused. When an investigator inserts their beliefs, explicitly or implicitly, into the case, a fair conclusion cannot be made.

Question Discussion

1. How do office staff ensure respect for minoritized students by helping make them comfortable in spaces reflective of harmful societal structures?
2. How do office staff reduce bias in their investigative proceedings to increase fairness for all accused students?
3. What work, if any, can be done to reduce the comparison between academic integrity offices and the justice system?
4. How do office staff reduce bias in their preparation for investigative proceedings?

Conclusion

Respect for and fairness towards students with minoritized social identities is important for ensuring students feel safe and supported as they move through office procedures.

Chapter 5
Responsibility

Chapter Contents:

Scaffolding Writing for an A
  Emilienne Idorenyin Akpan, American University of Nigeria, Nigeria
Statistically Surprising Standardized State-Wide Scores Sold
  Christian Moriarty, St. Petersburg College, United States
Baiting the Offender
  Valerie P. Denney, Embry-Riddle Aeronautical University, United States
One Size Fits All
  Sara Kellogg, Iowa State University, United States
Weighing the Options
  Sara Kellogg, Iowa State University, United States
Does Co-Authorship Imply a Responsibility for the Whole Document?
  Pamela Kennedy and Hans Kunov, University of Toronto, Canada
Alma Mater Should Always Matter
  Blaire N. Wilson and Jason T. Ciejka, Emory University, United States
Fake Grade Booster Classes
  Martin Daumiller, University of Augsburg, Germany
Abuse of Power by Medical Teachers: Can We Still Become Role Models?
  Ita Armyanti, Agustina Arundina Trihardja Tejoyuwono, and
  Muhammad Asroruddin, Universitas Tanjungpura, Indonesia
That's Not Fair: Balancing the Workload for Remote Teams
  Imani Akin and Gail Claybrooks, American College of Education, United States
Student's Legal Defense and Institutional Responsibility
  Christian Moriarty, St. Petersburg College, United States
Contract Cheating Coercion
  Christian Moriarty, St. Petersburg College, United States

Responsibility identifies that upholding the values of integrity is simultaneously an individual duty and a shared concern. Examples of responsibility in academic life include engaging in difficult conversations, knowing and following institutional rules and policies, holding yourself accountable for your actions, following through with tasks and expectations, and modeling good behavior. It is the idea of making sure that one is holding oneself accountable for their own actions. We also often want our students to take responsibility for their actions. To demonstrate this responsibility, we encourage all at the institution to first know the policies, but then to take responsibility to ask for clarification if needed. Responsibility is also creating understanding and respecting personal boundaries and following through. Just as students should take responsibility for the work they submit; faculty members are responsible for teaching our students and holding our students accountable. The faculty should also take responsibility for when things do not go quite as well as they planned with an assignment or maybe they were not quite as clear on their assignment guidelines. We also ask our institutions to take responsibility possibly through a long-term 5- or 10-year plan. These long-term plans allow for transparency of both successes and failures. There are 12 case studies in this book which address the primary value of responsibility.

Case Studies Focused on the Students. There are two case studies which primarily address this perspective.

In "Case 1: *Scaffolding Writing for an A*" students participate in a literacy program for non-native English speakers. For all exercises, students are permitted to self-correct common errors. Some students became more interested in perfect letter grades than in the learning process.

In "Case 2: *Statistically Surprising Standardized State-Wide Scores Sold*" 15 students in a healthcare program earned perfect or near-perfect scores on a state-wide, standardized practice test for a licensing exam. One of the students admits they received the answers from a classmate and gives screenshots of the emails between students sharing them.

Case Studies Focused on the Faculty. There are eight case studies which primarily address this perspective.

Two cases address so-called academic help websites. In "Case 3: *Baiting the Offender*" a professor suspects that some of her students are posting their completed assignments on a well-known help website. She considers posing as a student on the website and posting wrong answers in the hope of catching students in an integrity violation. In "Case 4: *One Size Fits All*" an instructor finds a number of her students have cheated using an academic help website. She indicates if students admit responsibility, they will have a lesser penalty, but if they deny responsibility, the penalty will be more severe.

Two cases address academic misconduct. In "Case 5: *Weighing the Options*" an instructor receives homework from two students that he suspects engaged in academic misconduct. When meeting with the two students individually, they present the information very differently, with one appearing remorseful and the other defensive and blaming. In "Case 6: *Does Co-Authorship Imply a Responsibility for the Whole Document?*" students submit a team assignment containing plagiarized material. In each case, the instructors ponder the appropriate response.

In "Case 7: *Alma Mater Should Always Matter*" a faculty member is serving on a search committee for an international fellowship. One student from her institution is a finalist for the award; however, she is concerned that the student is exaggerating her contributions.

In "Case 8: *Fake Grade Booster Classes*" a faculty member learned about her colleague, whose classes are apparently referred to as "GPA boosters" and all graded papers from the past semesters were an "A". The faculty member ponders what action to take.

In "Case 9: *Abuse of Power by Medical Teachers: Can We Still Become Role Models?*" a medical teacher supports her obligations to help and to give experiential learning to her students. However, the teacher does not have a medical license as a doctor, and she doesn't have the right to hold a vaccination clinic and receive money for the services.

In "Case 10: *That's Not Fair: Balancing the Workload for Remote Teams*" two members of the project management team noticed that they are often required to resolve conflicts and challenges a rising from a lack of accountability and inconsistency in leadership's decision-making. The arbitrary decision-making has created inequity and mistrust among team members.

Case Studies Focused on the Academic Integrity Office and Administration. There are two case studies which primarily address this perspective. In "Case 11: *Student's Legal Defense and Institutional Responsibility*" a student is accused of cheating on an online proctored exam. The institution's integrity office is contacted by an attorney representing the accused student and claims that the official process at the institution has not been followed and threatens a lawsuit.

In "Case 12: *Contract Cheating Coercion*" the dean of students is contacted by an anonymous individual claiming that a student is paying a contract cheating company to complete a course on the student's behalf. The individual is now following up on a threat to out the student for nonpayment.

In addition to the 12 case studies in this chapter on responsibility, 31 other case studies in this book address responsibility as a secondary value. Refer to that value chapter as shown for an introduction to each case study.

Honesty:

- *Buyers' Remorse*
- *Should I Pay the Contract Cheating Sites to Get the Answer?*
- *Caught in the Act*
- *Professor Purposely Publishes Student Paper Without Giving Credit*
- *A Syllabus Sleight of Hand*
- *Foiling Attempts to Facilitate File Sharing: Updating Assessments*
- *Readied Recalcitrance*

Trust:

- *Suspicious Success*
- *My Students, My Research Subjects—Trust in Faculty, Researcher, and Student Relationships*
- *What Do You Mean Students Are in Charge?*
- *Machine Learning: Trusting the Training Data, or the Trainer?*
- *Using Relational Coordination to Promote Academic Integrity*

Fairness:

- *Collusion Confusion*
- *Collusion by Coercion*
- *Higher Learning, Higher Stakes*
- *Flagrant Foul on the Faculty*
- *All for One and One for All*
- *It Doesn't Add Up*
- *Can't Put My Finger on It*
- *Socialize with Specialists to Spot and Stem Spinning*
- *Multi-use Presentations, "Retritos"*

Respect:

- *Time Is a Non-Renewable Resource*
- *Email Déjà Vu*
- *When the Bones Are Good: Laying the Foundation for Faculty*

Courage:

- *Don't Harm the Messenger*
- *But I Know This Student Well*
- *To Pursue or Not Pursue*
- *Taking a Stand for Integrity: A Whistleblower's Tale*
- *Demonstrating Courage to Stand for Integrity*
- *To Tell or Not to Tell: That Is the Question*
- *Self-Plagiarism in PhD Student's Thesis*

Case 1: Scaffolding Writing for an A

Emilienne Idorenyin Akpan, American University of Nigeria, Nigeria

Synopsis/Summary

Iwaun coordinates a literacy program for non-native English speakers in a liberal arts college. For all exercises, students use pencils to self-correct common errors. During essay writing, some students became more interested in perfect letter grades than in the learning process; and asked to do their assignment during their group study time. Iwaun provided a new prompt, but the students did not know that they would also attempt the same task in class after submitting the assignment.

Supporting Information

Academic writing is an important skill in a liberal arts education. However, for non-native speakers of English, this competency can seem daunting because it differs greatly from how peers usually express themselves or communicate with each other in familiar environments. The literacy program focuses on activities and drills that enhance sentence construction, mechanics, and paragraph building skills. The instructor also uses real student writing with relatable expressions to explain the lessons. In this class, students use pencils to correct common errors that they identify as instruction progresses. While having a good letter grade is important, the process in obtaining it through transferable skills matters too.

"I think we should be allowed to take the notebooks and do the exercises ending class," sighed Aisha.

"Allowed. After classes," Idanre spoke slowly.

"Noted," Aisha smiled.

"What is the hurry? We're learning at our level." Idanre erased a word and replaced it with a synonym. He had discovered how to use the dictionary for this purpose. Then he read the sentence slowly to himself.

"We should be trusted to do our work ourselves," Aisha frowned.

"By ourselves. Remember how 'shortcuts' caused Ebony and Abu to face the academic integrity council? Ms. Iwaun always encourages us to do the right thing and work honestly. She responds to all our questions and reminds us weekly about the Writing Center's tutorials. There's nothing wrong in learning from mistakes. I am improving," Idanre added.

"I would just like to have no mistakes for once," exhaled Aisha.

"Don't be tempted to submit what you cannot explain. We know why it is important to avoid misconduct. All our instructors share these guidelines with us in their syllabi on Canvas." Idanre closed his notebook, stood, and submitted his completed work to the instructor.

"Aisha," called Idanre as he pulled a chair, "let's revise your last sentence together."

Value Discussion

This case study highlights responsibility, accountability, and some of the challenges that non-native speakers of the English language face in higher education. We have (i) an institution with a structure which addresses violations of academic integrity, (ii) an instructor who takes the students through succeeding topics and tasks with the possibility of self-correcting as their knowledge of expectations develops and (iii) students who understand the need to apply the skills taught, do their assignments by themselves, and not sacrifice personal integrity for a "quick" outstanding letter grade that they cannot defend.

Fairness is a secondary value addressed in this case study. This means that class expectations and school policies apply to everyone in the same way. There are no waivers. The instructor has posted the school policy on misconduct on the course Canvas page and has explained the consequences of violations to the students. In addition, the Writing Center is also there to support students at any level. Furthermore, students are taught the relevant skills to avoid being tempted by quick fixes. The academic integrity council is also a reminder that learning is a developmental process for everyone. This value reinforces honesty, accountability, and personal integrity.

Respect is also addressed in this case study as a secondary value. It is important in a learning environment as it also influences the dynamics of interpersonal relationships. The instructor is accommodating, accessible and understanding towards the students. When students observe the academic integrity policies, they demonstrate self-respect, and regard for the school, their instructors, and their peers. Also, the instructor uses examples students can relate with to validate their experiences and this is also very important in a learning environment. Furthermore, the students work with each other courteously and listen to one another as they learn in different contexts. No one is made to feel incompetent.

Question Discussion

1. To what extent may regular college programs put too much pressure to succeed on students who are non-native speakers of the English language?
2. To what extent is the instructor's strategy to encourage responsibility during assignments ethical?
3. If an idea can be understood, must it be grammatically correct to earn a passing grade?
4. Discuss whether out-of-class assignments unconsciously encourage undue collaborations and contract cheating.

Conclusion

The foundation of developmental educational goals should build self-confidence, encourage personal integrity and hard work, promote responsibility, enhance accountability, and support the unbiased treatment of everyone through respect and fairness.

Case 2: Statistically Surprising Standardized State-Wide Scores Sold

Christian Moriarty, St. Petersburg College, United States

Synopsis/Summary

Fifteen students in a healthcare program earned perfect or near-perfect scores on a state-wide, standardized practice test for a licensing exam. When approached, one of the students admits they received the answers from a classmate and gives the professor screenshots of the emails between students sharing them. The originating student also admits to cheating, but claims they purchased the answers from a faculty member at another institution in the state.

Supporting Information

Academic Integrity Manager Waverly Haught has been recently made aware of a significant allegation of cheating. Tali Jenkins is a professor of nursing and is the primary instructor in charge of preparing nursing students to do well on their licensing examination. There is a practice test that all students in the state take in preparation for the exam, and they all take it at about the same time with the same questions.

Professor Jenkins was extremely surprised to discover fifteen of her students got near-perfect scores, which is statistically unlikely at best and evidence of something afoul at worst. She sent an email to every student who took the practice exam asking about information on these phenomena. One student comes forward admitting to receiving the questions and answers from another student and provides screenshots of the emails. Professor Jenkins then contacts that student who also immediately admits to sharing the answers with almost every student that did "too" well but admits something else: they purchased the questions and answers from a faculty member at a different nursing college within the state. They claim to be able to provide evidence of this fact upon request.

Academic Integrity Manager Waverly Haught needs to consider next steps, what sanctions or processes to pursue, and who to interview or investigate.

Value Discussion

It is the responsibility of students to learn with integrity, avoid cheating, and sometimes (depending on institutional honor codes or ethics arguments) report the wrongdoing of other students. This situation describes some of the most heinous types of cheating of collusion in a cheating ring through illicitly purchased answers to a serious exam. In turn, it is also the responsibility of institutions to investigate cheating and be transparent about its occurrence in order for trust in graduates' degrees to be legitimately earned. This is especially the case in healthcare programs, where a graduate is directly entrusted with peoples' lives.

Fairness is a secondary value addressed in this case study. It, of course, is not fair to all students for some to receive exam answers and some not, as it produces distrust in the examination and distrust that the results are valid. So, too, is it important for administrators and faculty members to pursue investigations fairly; are statistically improbable results on exams not in-themselves sufficient evidence of cheating? Evidence should be gathered before individuals or groups of students are punished, and each student should be granted appropriate due process separate from the other students.

Question Discussion

1. This is a large, substantial cheating ring and has implications across the program. As a faculty member or an integrity office administrator, how do you responsibly discuss this with the institutional community?
2. After an investigation is concluded, what responsibility does the institution have to prevent future occurrences? How can a cheating ring like this be prevented in the future?
3. What are the fairest repercussions or remedial measures for the originating student and the students that benefited from buying the answers?
4. How do you approach (and should you even!) the other institution where the faculty member that sold the answers teaches?

Conclusion

Alleged collusion rings necessitate significant care and expertise in investigation, fair sanctioning, and public communication to maintain responsibility, prevent future occurrences, maximize, and trust for all stakeholders.

Case 3: Baiting the Offender

Valerie P. Denney, Embry-Riddle Aeronautical University, United States

Synopsis/Summary

Martha is a professor at an accredited university in the US. She sees that some of her students are posting their completed assignments on a well-known study-resource website. The study-resource website is often used by students to copy answers. Martha considers posing as a student on the website and posting wrong answers in the hope of catching students in an integrity violation when students use the wrong answers in class.

Supporting Information

Students receive mixed messages from these so-called study-resource sites. On the one hand, these sites tout they provide resources to students when the instructor or university resources are not available. However, in practice, these sites are the next generation file cabinet of completed assignments which are often reused, in part or in whole as original submittals.

Martha is clearly frustrated by the proliferation of these companies and feels powerless to take action against the companies.

At a recent faculty meeting Martha exclaimed, "I am sick and tired of students cheating on my assignments. I need to take action—no matter what it takes. I can't fight these companies head on, so I'll fight fire with fire."

Kangela, another faculty member reacts with "No matter what it takes? Do you really mean that? How far are you willing to go?"

Titjana chimes in "All the way! What's wrong with posting some faulty information on these sites? When students use the information, we'll know where they got it from, and we can punish them for the cheaters they are!"

Martha agrees and says, "I already have a sample test with some well-placed wrong answers ready to go. Kangela, are you with us on this?"

Kangela looks away in disgust and says to himself, "But it isn't that simple."

Value Discussion

The primary value associated with this case study is responsibility. It is both an individual duty and a shared concern at educational institutions. Responsibility includes holding oneself accountable for actions and modeling good behavior. In this case, it would be easy to focus on the students' behavior in posting and using the material on the website. Posting material with the intent of trading or bartering assignments is clearly inappropriate behavior, but responsibility goes both ways. In this case study, we need to focus on the responsibility of the faculty members who have a duty to the institution, as well as themselves. How would the public react if it were known that faculty members are trying to trick students into being caught for cheating?

The secondary value in this case study is honesty. As a foundational element of integrity, one must be truthful and provide factual information. Deceit, including posting false information, is a slippery slope. Maybe it starts with something small, and one might think it is not a big deal or characterize it simply as a little white lie. But if the students and administration knew that the faculty were dishonest, would they be trusted in the future? Faculty credibility could be at stake. Faculty members need to set an example and model good behavior.

Question Discussion

1. How do principles of responsibility and honesty apply as they relate to this case study?
2. As a faculty member, what options does Martha have for combatting unauthorized use of her class material?
3. What role does the administration play in addressing Martha's proposed action?

Conclusion

Those entrusted with teaching students must model good behavior and demonstrate responsibility by holding oneself accountable when using the means to justify the end.

Case 4: One Size Fits All

Sara Kellogg, Iowa State University, United States

Synopsis/Summary

Dr. Flynn is an instructor at an American accredited university that finds a number of her students have cheated using a so-called academic help website. She contacts students with options for resolving the issue to help reduce time spent on a sizable referral to the student conduct office. She indicates if students admit responsibility, they will have a lesser penalty, but if they deny responsibility, the penalty will be more severe.

Supporting Information

Lucy, Dr. Flynn's TA, has begun grading a recent quiz from the statistics course and notices an odd incorrect answer by a student on one of the questions. After grading a few more quizzes and finding a similar answer, Lucy recognizes a pattern. She pulls out 26 student quizzes that have similar nonsensical answers, and being familiar with online help platforms, does an internet search for the question and answer, finding it at one of these websites. Lucy contacts Dr. Flynn to share this information. Dr. Flynn is shocked and frustrated that so many students would cheat. She is also worried about how much work it would be to refer all these students to the student conduct office, as she has a number of other courses to teach. Dr. Flynn consults with some colleagues who sympathize with her but don't have helpful advice. She decides the easiest path might be to use leverage to get students to admit their misconduct. Dr. Flynn emails all of the students and shares, "I am aware and have evidence that a number of you engaged in academic misconduct on the last statistics quiz. If you respond to this email and admit responsibility, you will get a zero on the quiz, but will be permitted to stay in the course. However, if you deny responsibility, you will be referred to the student conduct office and will fail the course."

Value Discussion

Responsibility is the primary value when evaluating this case. While students are expected to demonstrate academic integrity, faculty also promote this by taking the appropriate steps to ensure this behavior is addressed equitably and consistently. Using the university policy developed to address misconduct supports all students and faculty by ensuring objective processes of accountability and appropriate response.

Question Discussion

1. Is it appropriate for the faculty to use this type of strategy as a resolution process?
2. How might this type of approach have a disparate impact on some students?
3. What other strategies could faculty use to effectively address this type of large group misconduct?

Conclusion

When navigating even the more time-consuming referrals for misconduct, faculty have a responsibility to utilize university processes that ensure student's rights, which will also further support faculty academic decisions.

Case 5: Weighing the Options

Sara Kellogg, Iowa State University, United States

Synopsis/Summary

Aaron is an instructor at an American accredited university and receives homework from two students that he suspects engaged in academic misconduct. When meeting with the two students individually, they present very differently, with one appearing remorseful and the other defensive and blaming. Based on their responses, Aaron is considering showing leniency in his grading to the more remorseful student.

Supporting Information

While grading an assignment in his physics course, Aaron notes that Shawn and Jamie have some similar incorrect answers, unique to the two of them. Aaron schedules meetings to discuss his suspicion of academic misconduct. Aaron meets first with Shawn, who breaks down and tearfully states, "I am so sorry I let you down. I struggle with anxiety and this semester has been hard, as my grandmother passed away." Shawn shares he fell behind so asked a friend for help, but knows they went too far. He shares his hope that Aaron doesn't see him as a horrible person. Aaron's meeting with Jamie was very different. Aaron asked Jamie to explain what happened, and Jamie appeared agitated, stating angrily, "I cannot believe I am in trouble for simply helping a friend in need. My work was done and all I did was help Shawn understand some of the problems. I didn't cheat." Jamie continued, defensively sharing that the course was difficult, and Aaron's lectures were not helpful. Aaron agreed the course was rigorous but countered that this incident appeared to be more than him just offering Shawn simple assistance, to which Jamie retorted, "I basically had to teach Shawn the subject because you didn't!" After the meetings, Aaron weighs his options. Aaron's inclination is to let Shawn redo the assignment for partial credit since he was remorseful and indicated he'd experienced a personal crisis. Aaron considers giving Jamie a zero, since he was defensive and rude, and Aaron doesn't believe Jamie has learned anything from this incident.

Value Discussion

The primary value seen in this case is responsibility. Faculty have a responsibility to enforce course policies equitably and may benefit from consideration or reflection on how individual student personalities and responses might affect their objectivity. Students have a responsibility to acknowledge when they have engaged in misconduct, and respectfully share any course concerns they might have.

Fairness is a secondary value in this case. Faculty may be challenged by certain student personalities or responses and may benefit from relying more heavily on course policies and procedures in order to ensure fairness during those times.

Question Discussion

1. Should students suspected of academic misconduct be required or expected to admit responsibility and demonstrate remorse for the misconduct?

2. When determining academic outcomes for misconduct, how much consideration should be given to a student's individual emotional response or demonstrated remorse?
3. What types of academic outcomes and responses would you recommend Aaron take with these students?

Conclusion

While certain incidents may provide challenges to a faculty's empathy and patience, there remains a responsibility to administer course policies objectively and conscientiously.

Case 6: Does Co-Authorship Imply a Responsibility for the Whole Document?

Pamela Kennedy and Hans Kunov, University of Toronto, Canada

Synopsis/Summary

Three students submit a team assignment containing plagiarized material. The fundamental principle we apply is that if you put your name on a document you are responsible for its entirety. This holds for all levels of academia, and society at large. Students are frequently under time pressure and plagiarized material can slip by other members of the group. Should each team member be sanctioned, including those who were not directly involved in plagiarism? Strong mitigating factors may reduce the sanction.

Supporting Information

In academia, intellectual property is produced mainly in the form of scholarly papers, lecture material, and papers written for course requirements. Plagiarism in academia is a serious matter. Using another's words or ideas without proper attribution, even when done unintentionally, is a form of academic dishonesty. Patents, trademarks, and copyrights are legal protections; however, plagiarism continues to occur. It is the responsibility of the author(s) of any paper to make sure the contents are ethically sound. All intellectual properties need to be respected.

Three students, accused of submitting plagiarized material in their group assignment, are interviewed separately by the AI officer.

STUDENT 1:	I'm sorry, professor. The document does contain copied material. My teammate told me he copied from an online source. I guess this means we all get punished?
STUDENT 2:	My teammate may have used plagiarized code on his part, but I did not plagiarize. I had no knowledge of this. Also, how am I supposed to find out?
STUDENT 3:	I know there is plagiarized material. I was struggling and didn't know what else to do, so I found code online. I told one of my teammates, but not the other.
AI OFFICER (SAME RESPONSE TO EACH STUDENT):	When your name is on a document, submitted for credit in this case, you are responsible for its contents. A signature signifies an agreement, and you have a responsibility to make sure the contents do not violate the rules. You must communicate with your team members and scrutinize the document you are signing.

Value Discussion

It is the responsibility of each author, including those who contributed minimally, to make sure the contents were produced fairly, honestly, and ethically, void of plagiarism. The students in this case study may question how to avoid plagiarism in group work. Develop a rapport, strong communication, and trust within the group, discuss the concept of plagiarism, and agree to work with integrity. Individual assignments can pose their own challenges. In an engineering environment, where collaboration is encouraged, understanding how to collaborate without plagiarizing is key. Discuss ideas with classmates but write the paper independently.

Fairness and honesty are two of the other most important attributes outlined in the International Center for Academic Integrity's definition. Many universities follow this definition in their Code. Both attributes are fundamental to a successful and well-functioning society as well as in situations of smaller scale. This case illustrates the importance of both, amongst peers, whereby members of the group are relying on each other to act with academic honesty. Group work is beneficial as members of differing strengths share ideas, creating an effective learning environment. Could individual contributions be identified and assembled by an editor? In that case, is the editor responsible?

Question Discussion

1. Are students excluded from the general principle of joint responsibility? Are they expected to work as they will in their future profession? To what degree should university or professional schools instruct students in professional ethics?
2. Is "I did not know my teammate plagiarized some material, and don't know how I would be able to check for it" an acceptable excuse?
3. Should a sanction be adjusted for the degree of or knowledge of involvement?
4. What is the significance of your signature or co-authorship? In some cases, well-known scientists have surreptitiously been added as authors to papers for added prestige and ease of peer review.
5. Intellectual property is the main product in academia. Are we, as academics, too obsessed with IP?

Conclusion

Authors are responsible for the contents of their work. Co-authors must be able to trust that contributions were produced responsibly and with integrity; something fundamental to fair and effective co-authorship.

Case 7: Alma Mater Should Always Matter

Blaire N. Wilson and Jason T. Ciejka, Emory University, United States

Synopsis/Summary

Maxine, an alumna of Decatur University, is serving on a search committee for a prestigious international fellowship. She is excited to see that a student from her institution is a finalist for the award; however, in reviewing Veronica's CV and statement of purpose, she is concerned that the student is exaggerating her contributions. Maxine is uncertain about whether to mention this to the committee members, contact the institution, or overlook her serious suspicions in case she is wrong.

Supporting Information

In her CV, Veronica lists that she was an ambassador for the Alumni and Engagement Office (AEO). As part of this role, she indicated that she led the university's initiative for the popular "Thank a Donor" Day. Her CV states that she is also the recruitment chair for the ambassador program and in charge of marketing and communications for the group.

Maxine is directly connected to some of the organizations and activities that are listed on Veronica's CV. As an active alumna, she is a contributor to several different scholarships at Decatur University, even endowing a scholarship of her own that awards $4,000 to an out-of-state student. Through her work with the AEO and her knowledge of its programs, Maxine is deeply concerned that Veronica has inflated some of her responsibilities and has provided misleading titles of her leadership positions.

In a conversation with a staff member at the AEO, Maxine recently asked how the ambassador program was going; the staff member responded, "It's a strong group of students right now, but we are looking to grow the program so I've been coordinating the recruiting efforts by meeting with different academic departments, posting to the group's social media, and reviewing scholarship recipients who also show leadership potential." The staff member continued, "Undergraduate students are so busy that they just haven't helped out as much as we would like."

Maxine also received a thank you card in the mail for a recent donation. The card was signed by the AEO ambassadors; it showed eleven names, but not Veronica's.

A colleague on the search committee has come by Maxine's office and playfully comments, "Wow! Your alma mater is a strong contender!" Maxine is unsure how to respond and feels uneasy given her concerns.

Value Discussion

Responsibility is the primary value in this case. Engaging in difficult conversations is one component of the value of responsibility. Though many individuals avoid difficult conversations, they can be rewarding. Such conversations can lead to a newly found common ground between individuals. While this scenario is not inherently focused on academic integrity in the classroom, it does speak to the broader values of integrity and how students' contributions to co-curricular and extracurricular activities impact the reputation of the institution and its integrity.

A secondary value in this case is honesty. In an application to an external opportunity such as a fellowship or internship, students have a responsibility to present their experiences in an accurate and honest way. Committee members and programs that encounter inaccurate or misleading materials should address the suspicions by seeking more information; otherwise, they risk perpetuating the dishonesty and undermining the credibility of the opportunity.

Question Discussion

1. How might Maxine address the discrepancies in Veronica's CV?
2. What should Maxine do next? Should she contact the applicant directly? Notify their institution? Share their concerns with the committee?
3. How do institutions encourage students to present themselves in an honest and transparent way and fight pressures to exaggerate and mislead?

Conclusion

Alumni have a responsibility to their institution to promote honesty and integrity and preserve the value of the degree, which may mean holding a student accountable.

Case 8: Fake Grade Booster Classes

Martin Daumiller, University of Augsburg, Germany

Synopsis/Summary

Amanda is a faculty member at a Canadian university. In discussions with her students about the standards expected in her classes, Amanda learned about her colleague, Sophie Collins, whose classes are apparently referred to as "GPA boosters." After investigating further, Amanda found that her colleague had neither meeting times nor syllabi assigned for her classes and had graded all papers from the past semesters with an "A."

Supporting Information

When going over the assignments Amanda expects her students to fulfill, she explained, the details of her expectations and grading. Student 1 said, "This is such a joke! For Miss Collins' class, students don't even have to work for a good grade." Student 2 laughed: "Well, not everyone can fiddle their way through university with GPA boosters—at least we get to learn something, right?"

Students love to talk about their lecturers, but something made Amanda suspicious. After class, she spoke to administration and looked into the study forum of her colleague and could neither find a syllabus, nor any information on classes that would have taken place. In the course of further research, Amanda found her students to have been right in their assumptions—in the last three semesters, students who participated in Miss Collins' classes did not receive anything worse than an A. Working herself up about this information, Amanda tried to think of the right thing to do.

Value Discussion

The primary value for this case is responsibility. Being a member of an academic community does not only include preparing and giving classes and conducting research. It also involves the task of guarding values and teaching the meaning of "academic integrity." In this context, it is not enough to communicate values like truthfulness and reliability in class. In their function as role model, a faculty member needs to be someone students can look up to: Someone who is consistent in their academic ideals, stands up against wrongdoings, and is not afraid of engaging in difficult conversations with students or colleagues if need be.

Fairness, a secondary value, is a key component in academic education. It is the duty of faculty members to treat their students and each other fairly to maintain the ideal of impartial treatment. This includes talking to students and being transparent about expectations and methods. Trust within an academic community can only be built if educational fairness is established through standing by these expectations and evaluating accurately and impartially in accordance with them. Being consistent and just in cases of academic integrity breaches is essential to maintaining fairness in an academic environment.

Question Discussion

1. What ethical standards are breached when offering such "GPA booster" classes?
2. What role does the administration play in such classes being offered?
3. How should Amanda communicate about this colleague with her students?
4. What should Amanda do about her colleague, and how can the integrity office help?

Conclusion

Faculty members have the responsibility to communicate and model proper behavior and expectations students have to meet, while enforcing fair teaching conditions for all students.

Case 9: Abuse of Power by Medical Teachers: Can We Still Become Role Models?

Ita Armyanti, Agustina Arundina Trihardja Tejoyuwono, and Muhammad Asroruddin, Universitas Tanjungpura, Indonesia

Synopsis/Summary

Mrs. Honest is one of the medical teachers at an accredited university in Indonesia. She believes that she has obligations to help and to give experiential learning to her students. However, Mrs. Honest does not have a medical license as a doctor, and she doesn't have the right to hold a vaccination clinic for Hepatitis B for pre-clerkship medical students. Additionally, she collected money for its services and uses unlicensed clerkship students as vaccinators, without supervision.

Supporting Information

The case appeared when the pre-clerkship medical students asked their supervisors about the second vaccination for Hepatitis B that had already been scheduled by Mrs. Honesty. The medical education program manager is shocked with this information. They try to collect more detailed data from other pre-clerkship students, and they are surprised by what they find.

MEDICAL TEACHER A:	So, for a long time you have been vaccinated by your own friend without supervision from Mrs. Honest and you paid for it?
STUDENT B:	Not only me Ma'am, but the other group that have entered the clerkship since last year are doing the same, Ma'am.
MEDICAL TEACHER A:	How can you trust her so easily?
STUDENT A:	She is our teacher, right Ma'am? And she is always kind with us. We didn't know that she doesn't have a medical permit to do that, and she always says if we try to do injections with each other, we can be more advanced as medical doctors in the future.
MEDICAL TEACHER B:	And you always believe what she said to you? Even the vaccination is not held in the proper places, like in the hospital. Do you realize that the vaccination held in the backyard garden at our building, is not a proper place, and not safe for us?
STUDENT B:	We think its OK Ma'am, as long as that Mrs. Honest said so. We think that we were in the middle of our education, and because she is our teacher, we believe her.

| MEDICAL TEACHER A: | And you paid for it? It wasn't free? And your classmates as your vaccinator without supervision? |
| STUDENT A: | We thought it would be fine, and until now, there were no complications or other complaints from our friends. |

Value Discussion

The primary value for this case is responsibility. Following institutional and government rules makes us more accountable for our actions. It is also the fundamental principle of role modeling as a medical teacher. As a faculty member, one must accept this obligation. The role modeling learning method is an important process in medical education. This occurs when the faculty are able to demonstrate clinical skills, act as an example (role model), articulate their opinions and behave with a professional attitude. This learning process can occur at all stages of the curriculum, ranging from formal, informal, and hidden.

The secondary value for this case is respect. Recognizing that respect is reciprocal and also acknowledges the consequences of our actions and words on others, the faculty must be aware of this obligation. Respect for others is recognized as an essential attribute of medical professionalism. Respect in the medical profession is a central humanistic value that physicians should hold and apply; it also consists of valued relational/interactional acts of one person towards another. Respect is related to positive attitudes towards human worth and the dignity of every individual. Medical educators emphasize the need to treat medical students with respect because it models for them what is expected of them as physicians in interactions with vulnerable others.

Question Discussion

1. Why should responsibility be taught in the medical professionalism formation?
2. As role model medical teachers, how can they approach this?
3. As a role model medical teacher, one must show that the students are equal. What is your argument?

Conclusion

The medical professionalism learning process teaches our students to be able to establish a good social contract with our society. The responsibility and respect for others, is the basis of professional behavior.

Case 10: That's Not Fair: Balancing the Workload for Remote Teams

Imani Akinand Gail Claybrooks, American College of Education, United States

Synopsis/Summary

Jeannie and Johnnie are part of a five-member project management team working remotely for the academic excellence department in an online university. They noticed that they are often required to resolve conflicts and challenges arising from a lack of accountability and inconsistency in leadership's decision-making. The arbitrary decision-making has created inequity and mistrust among team members.

Supporting Information

The project management team has weekly meetings to discuss issues, problem-solve, and create best practices for faculty instruction. The institution is faced with a challenge of how to best manage faculty accountability during the period deemed as the Great Resignation period. When issues arise involving faculty, the team leader decides Jeannie and Johnnie should complete the deficient tasks rather than requiring the responsible faculty to complete the work out of fear of faculty attrition. The work puts an extra strain on Jeannie and Johnnie, resulting in frequent seven-day work weeks. Other team members are not directed to perform these tasks.

During one of the weekly team meetings, Jeannie said, "Why do I have to be the one who fixes or performs faculty's work for which they receive credit?" Johnnie chimes in and says, "I agree with Jeannie, why do I have to be the fail-safe for faculty? Why do I have to clean up work for which others have been paid to complete?"

Jeannie says, "Yes, Dr. Strangelove, who is tenured faculty, always submits what he calls a finished project and upon leadership review, it's not complete, then *I'm* responsible for getting the project done, yet everyone thanks him." Johnnie says, "I want to have time to enjoy my family, too, and not work long nights and weekends. Why can't the decision-making include redirecting the responsibility back to faculty to ensure equity in workloads so that all team members can have a work-life balance?"

Value Discussion

The primary value addressed in this case study is responsibility. Team members are responsible for individual and team performance. Remote work has gained momentum as companies have come to value this process. Online leadership teams need harmony and collaboration to achieve program objectives and student learning outcomes. A team's effectiveness impacts the quality of service to faculty and students. Academic leadership teams should model behaviors expected of the stakeholders it serves. Fostering accountability and transparency are critical elements of team building. Team members must perform their tasks to ensure project success and maintain a healthy work environment. Shared responsibility is crucial to a healthy environment and work culture.

A secondary value addressed in this case study is fairness. The faculty roles are clearly delineated, and policies exist detailing faculty expectations yet when faculty do not follow policy, then Jeannie and Johnnie are asked to perform the work. Other team members are not required to take on additional tasks. The leadership decisions are reactive without consideration of consequences to the team members. Jeannie and Johnnie feel like scapegoats while leadership may feel that they are making the best decision for a swift resolution. Other team members may be able to contribute but feel Jeannie and Johnnie are favored by leadership.

The final secondary value addressed in this case study is trust. Inconsistent decision-making by team leaders has created an environment of mistrust and inequity among the team. Members are encouraged to be innovative and share best practices. Yet, Jeannie and Johnnie have noticed that projects developed collaboratively by the team are sometimes presented as being authored by the team leaders. Jeannie and Johnnie are becoming reluctant to collaborate or engage in discussions.

Question Discussion

1. What strategies can be implemented to promote responsibility, fairness and trust for a healthy team culture?
2. What are the benefits of teams adopting a decision-making model to support department processes?
3. What are the systemic effects for an organization when individual lack of responsibility creates inequities among team members?

Conclusion

More institutions should incorporate decision-making models to promote responsibility and fairness among remote teams to hold each other accountable and enhance trust in the execution of the organization's strategic goals.

Case 11: Student's Legal Defense and Institutional Responsibility

Christian Moriarty, St. Petersburg College, United States

Synopsis/Summary

A student is accused of cheating on an online proctored exam. It can be seen on video that there is some small evidence of the student using a disallowed resource. The institution's integrity office is contacted by an attorney representing the accused student. The attorney also emails the office making claims that the official process at your institution has not been followed, threatens a lawsuit, and demands for the integrity accusation to be dropped entirely.

Supporting Information

Academic Integrity Manager Jane Shephard, working for Nos Astra University, caught a stress-inducing case. A rather standard report came in from a professor alleging that a student of theirs, Donny Costa, was accessing what must be a phone or other electronic device during a closed-book online proctored exam. Manager Shephard has been provided the video of the student taking the exam and noted that it does appear that Danny is looking down into his lap periodically and answering questions immediately after, but it's not exactly definitive that he's accessing a phone or device.

What was not standard is that a few days after the allegation came in, the integrity office assistant was contacted by Elias Massani, claiming to be a hired attorney for Donny Costa and is inquiring about the institutional process of academic integrity violations at Nos Astra. Having been trained on privacy policy and law, the assistant refused all questions and directed Massani to email Shephard directly.

Shephard subsequently receives an email from Massani making several statements and demands:

1. He is upset the assistant did not answer his questions and claims this is an unfair delay to his client.
2. Claims that he accessed the process posted on Nos Astra's website and cites provisions that have allegedly not been followed to this point in Donny's case.
3. Demands that when and if a hearing occurs that he be present and able to speak at the hearing. He recognizes this is disallowed in Nos Astra's policy but says an exception should be made because Donny is facing "the academic death penalty."
4. Finally, if the charges are not dropped entirely, Massani reserves the right to sue Nos Astra, the professor, and Shephard personally.

Value Discussion

The primary value discussed in this case study is responsibility. Institutions of education have a responsibility to pursue accusations of academic integrity violations to defend the value of their degrees. They equally have a responsibility to follow their own rules and jurisdictional laws carefully and equally across all students, whether an attorney threatens a lawsuit or not. Institutions appropriately equipped with trained integrity managers and competent attorneys of their own should not be intimidated or drop investigations from threats of a lawsuit.

A secondary value described in this case study is fairness. All integrity investigations should be fair, and all cases should be treated the same whether the student has an attorney or not. Institutional policies should be written with the anticipation of legal involvement and should treat students identically whether they have them or not. Students who cannot afford attorneys should not be at a disadvantage in integrity processes.

Honesty is the other secondary value described in this case study. It is important to remember that attorneys have a fiduciary duty to their clients. While they may sometimes act in such a way that feels dishonest, attorneys are barred from directly lying in pursuit of their clients' goals by their licensure's code of ethics. Students, of course, should be honest in their dealings with their professors, the institution, and attorneys they hire.

Question Discussion

1. What are the institutional responsibilities to communicate with outside attorneys in the most ethical and legal ways?
2. How do you assure that a process is fair, and a student is not given preferential treatment in the process due to having an attorney? How do you make sure students who do NOT have attorneys get the full benefits of your process despite them not having lawyers?
3. How can hearings and processes encourage honesty?
4. How much should the legal department of your institution be involved after a lawyer contacts you?

Conclusion

While attorney participation in academic integrity cases can be daunting, it is the responsibility of integrity professionals to maintain processes to be consistent and just no matter their involvement.

Case 12: Contract Cheating Coercion

Christian Moriarty, St. Petersburg College, United States

Synopsis/Summary

The Dean of Students David Anderson is contacted by an anonymous stranger. They are claiming that one of your students, Jeff Moreau, is paying a contract cheating company to complete a course on the student's behalf. Worse, the stranger claims *they* are the contract cheating provider and Jeff didn't pay in full. The stranger is now following up on a threat to out the student for nonpayment and has screenshots of emails between the contract cheating provider and the student.

Supporting Information

The dean of students of Nos Astra University, David Anderson, received an email from an address he does not recognize and seems to be from out of the country. This is further evidenced by the English in the body of the email, which is imperfect but decent, as if written by someone that picked it up recently or uses it irregularly. It reads (sic):

"your'e student jeff moreau cheater in composition. no pay for service of writing. told wed tell you. Your welcome."

Seeing the irony of a potential cheater in composition class cheating through someone without a firm grasp of grammar, Dean Anderson noticed the email also had several picture attachments. One was a partial transcript of a text conversation of someone asking for papers to be written for them and negotiating price. Another is an unredacted credit card receipt, full numbers and CVV code, including the name "Edi Moreau," for a charge of 100 dollars. A handful more are partial screenshots of what looks like essays for a class. The final is what looks like an emailed demand for additional payment from the anonymous stranger addressed to a non-university address "JokerN7@omega.com"

Jane Shephard, the integrity office manager, is assigned the case to hash out. To Shephard, the essays do look like answers to prompts given at Nos Astra classes. She doesn't recognize the name Edi Moreau, but it is the same last name as the supposedly accused student. She also notes that this would be evidence of some payment, and based on the transcript, the person may have paid as agreed, so either more services were contracted, or the person is being blackmailed.

Value Discussion

The responsibility of administrators to maintain integrity at all education institutions is necessary to retain trust in the value of the degrees being offered. While it is difficult and uncomfortable to investigate someone being potentially blackmailed, it can be, and must be, done with compassion and justice. Appropriate rules must be enforced; or not if there is insufficient evidence. So, too, is there the responsibility of students to work and learn with integrity, and to hold themselves to account when they have committed wrongdoing.

To be honest in this situation, the integrity office manager must acknowledge that while this email doesn't look good for the student, the evidence isn't definitive. Good integrity investigations require an open mind and follow where the evidence leads. If there is insufficient evidence to show responsibility, officers must be honest with that showing. The student must be honest and forthcoming with the fact they have cheated. While this may especially be hard at this point, integrity demands it. Not to mention the sanction may be less severe. Of course, if indeed they cheated at all!

Question Discussion

1. What is the most responsible way to investigate an accusation of contract cheating services?
2. To what extent should a provider of evidence, who is an unethical actor in and of themselves, be relied upon?
3. What is the most appropriate remedial action to take after potential confirmation of this contract cheating?
4. Irony aside, is it ethical and/or appropriate to use this situation as a lesson for other students at the institution?

Conclusion

Students who purchase contract cheating services are at risk of blackmail if they do not pay or pay additional money after threats of exposure. Responsible investigatory methods should be used to determine the facts and appropriate sanctions.

Chapter 6
Courage

Chapter Contents:

Don't Harm the Messenger
  Sara Kellogg, Iowa State University, United States
To Tell or Not to Tell: That Is the Question
  Greg Preston, University of Newcastle, Australia
Mock Police Board Exam Puts Students in the Hot Seat
  Page C. Spiess, Norwich University, United States
Courage with Coding
  Jillian Orfeo, University of Maryland, United States
But I Know This Student Well
  Blaire N. Wilson and Jason T. Ciejka, Emory University, United States
To Pursue or Not Pursue
  Kaela Lindquist and Sharisse Stafford, University of North Carolina at Charlotte, United States
The Handy Dandy Dictionary
  Christian Moriarty, St. Petersburg College, United States
The Blackmail Blues
  Greg Preston, University of Newcastle, Australia
Taking a Stand for Integrity: A Whistleblower's Tale
  Shiva Sivasubramaniam, University of Derby, United Kingdom
Demonstrating Courage to Stand for Integrity
  Shiva Sivasubramaniam, University of Derby, United Kingdom
Self-Plagiarism in PhD Student's Thesis
  Tatjana Odineca and Ilze Birzniece, Riga Technical University, Latvia

Courage differs from the preceding fundamental values by being more a quality or capacity of character. However, as with each of the values, courage can be practiced and developed. Courage often is interpreted as a lack of fear. In reality, courage is the capacity to act in accordance with one's values despite fear. Examples of courage include being brave when others might not, taking a stand to address wrongdoing, being willing to take risk and risk failure, and being undaunted in defending integrity. One might need courage to be able to act in accordance with the other values. The previous five values sometimes can be intimidating, and one must have the courage to live out the value. For a student to speak up to their peers takes quite a bit of courage, or for our faculty members (especially prior to tenure) to stand up for what they think or what they believe in takes courage. We encourage all to have that voice to be able to take a stand, address wrongdoing, and understand there might be some discomfort but if you are standing up for the good, for something that you believe in, then it is worth it in the end. We ask our institutions to have courage just to make statements against wrongdoing. We have seen numerous current societal issues, and we encourage our institutions to take a stand to describe the culture and the community wanted at the institution. The courage in turn will continue to develop those previous five fundamental values. The six values will then lead to a high level of academic integrity culture at the institution.

There are 11 case studies in this book which address the primary value of courage.

Case Studies Focused on the Student. There are four case studies which primarily address this perspective.

Two of the cases deal with having information about misconduct of other students. In "Case 1: *Don't Harm the Messenger*" students have been sharing questions and answers about an upcoming quiz in a group chat. One student approaches the instructor with that information, but now the instructor wants the student to provide the names of the guilty parties. In "Case 2: *To Tell or Not to Tell: That Is the Question*" students have been discussing methods for circumventing academic integrity procedures at the university they attend. One student considers telling the instructor about the misconduct, but she is concerned about reprisals from other students.

One case addresses misconduct during oral exams. In "Case 3: *Mock Police Board Exam Puts Students in the Hot Seat*." After the first student in a one-on-one verbal exam finished, she shared the exam questions with her peers, which is prohibited. Only the last student had the courage to admit that he had the topic prior to the exam.

The final case study focused on the student perspective is called "Case 4: *Courage with Coding*." Here, a computer science student asks for help from the instructor on a recently graded assignment. While no additional guidance was given, the student was given the opportunity to redo the assignment. Frustrated, the student submitted an assignment found on the internet. When confronted with misconduct by the instructor, the student admits the wrongdoing while describing the stigma of asking for help.

Case Studies Focused on the Faculty and/or Academic Integrity Office. There are four case studies which primarily address this perspective.

Three of the cases address the right course of action the faculty member is struggling over. In "Case 5: *But I Know This Student Well*," a professor discovers plagiarism in an essay submitted by a student who has had a stressful semester and is applying to graduate school. In "Case 6: *To Pursue or Not Pursue*" several students appeared to collaborate on the final exam without permission and submitted nearly identical computer code. The instructor is struggling because of administrative pressure not to fail international students which would result in removal from the program and visa cancellation. In "Case 7: *The Handy Dandy Dictionary*" a student turns in a paper with strange language. The professor suspects misconduct and the use of a synonym replacement tool to hide plagiarism.

The case study titled "Case 8: *The Blackmail Blues*" addresses decision-making. Here, a student approaches the academic integrity office and admits to using an essay mill service for two assignments. The student is being blackmailed by the essay mill who are demanding additional payments to ensure that the university doesn't find out about their previous conduct.

Case Studies Focused on Researchers. There are three case studies which primarily address the researcher perspectives.

In "Case 9: *Taking a Stand for Integrity: A Whistleblower's Tale*," a faculty member found out that two other academics were using each other as reviewers for their papers to receive favorable decisions. The faculty member reported this to retraction watch which resulted in the manuscripts being retracted by many journal editors. In retaliation, the faculty member received threatening attempts to hinder her academic progression. In "Case 10: *Demonstrating Courage to Stand for Integrity*" an inexperienced researcher was ready to submit his first scientific manuscript as a senior author. The head of research wants his name listed as co-senior author, even though he did not contribute other than in review, to increase the chances of his paper being accepted. In "Case 11: *Self-Plagiarism in Ph.D. Student's Thesis*" a respected member of the scientific community finished his second PhD thesis. A plagiarism detection tool shows the compilation of almost fully copy-pasted parts of published papers which are not always cited. The review commission members are not willing to doubt the academic integrity of a colleague.

In addition to the 11 case studies in this chapter on courage, six other case studies in this book address courage as a secondary value. Refer to that value chapter as shown for an introduction to each case study.

Honesty:

- *Buyers' Remorse*
- *Photoshop: The Easiest (Worst!) Way Out*
- *A Syllabus Sleight of Hand*

Trust:

- *My Students, My Research Subjects—Trust in Faculty, Researcher, and Student Relationships*
- *Pressure vs. Courage: The Dean's Dilemma*

Fairness:

- *Multi-use Presentations, "Retritos"*

Case 1: Don't Harm the Messenger

Sara Kellogg, Iowa State University, United States

Synopsis/Summary

Olena is enrolled in a course at an American accredited university and approaches the instructor after class, sharing a course group chat that involves a majority of course enrollees where students are sharing questions and answers about an upcoming quiz. The instructor asks

Olena to identify all students involved in this chat. Olena is concerned about retaliation, but her instructor indicates she must share this information or face consequences.

Supporting Information

Olena is enrolled in a challenging Calculus course. A classmate adds Olena to a large group chat created to discuss the course. Olena receives a notification and sees that another student has posted questions and answers for an upcoming quiz in the chat. Olena is concerned about having any association with this, so leaves the group and contacts her Calculus professor, Dr. Burns. When they meet, Olena tells Dr. Burns about the group chat, showing him a screenshot of the quiz post, and sharing that she felt she needed to report this.

Dr. Burns is very upset and asks Olena to send him screenshots of the chat conversations and help him identify the students involved. Olena agrees to share the screenshots, but admits she is worried about how other students might respond if she shares individual students' names. Olena suggests, "Can't you just let the class know you are aware of the chat, and tell them it needs to stop, so that they don't find out I turned the group chat in?" Dr. Burns shares with Olena his appreciation of her coming forward, but indicates he really needs the names of the students involved so he can address this misconduct. Dr. Burns adds, "They may have done this before and may not stop unless I address them directly." When Olena continues to hesitate, Dr. Burns informs her that she must either provide the information, or she will be referred to the student conduct office.

Value Discussion

Courage is the primary value in this case. Students may demonstrate courage in upholding standards of academic integrity, but this doesn't negate related fears, and these may also need to be addressed. Faculty may need to be proactive and creative in their approaches to discussing and addressing everyone's responsibility to promote academic integrity in order to motivate students to take action when they identify misconduct occurring.

The value of responsibility can also be seen within this case. Students have a responsibility to themselves and their peers to uphold standards of academic integrity and address misconduct when observed. Faculty have a responsibility to acknowledge concerns and risks students may encounter and identify or recommend support where it is warranted.

Question Discussion

1. Should Olena's concerns about how other students might respond if she provides the names involved in the misconduct be considered by the faculty?
2. If she had concerns about possible retaliation for reporting, why would Olena choose to report the misconduct in the first place?
3. What impactful approach might faculty take in addressing this type of group misconduct?

Conclusion

Students willing to demonstrate courage in reporting peers engaged in academic misconduct may also have reasonable expectations to be safeguarded from significant repercussions.

Case 2: To Tell or Not to Tell: That Is the Question

Greg Preston, University of Newcastle, Australia

Synopsis/Summary

Sally approaches a member of the faculty, Dr. Bell, with a series of screenshots of a social media chat between two classmates. The classmates, Pat and Jo, are discussing methods for circumventing academic integrity procedures at the university they attend. The screenshots include evidence that Pat and Jo have both cheated on multiple previous assignments. While Sally is keen to do "the right thing" she is very worried about reprisals from the other students if it becomes known that she has informed the university. The screenshots are currently the only evidence of misconduct and could only have come from Sally.

Supporting Information

Three students, Pat, Jo and Sally, have been in the same cohort as they have worked their way through their degree. While not close friends, they have agreed to form a study group to work on a course that has a reputation of being "difficult" to pass. They form a private group chat on a social media site, WhatsApp. On that private group chat, Pat and Jo have had discussions about how to avoid doing their own work and discuss working with an assignment mill to create assignments. Both Jo and Pat discuss how they have used these assignment mills in the past, they both name specific courses that they have used assignment mills for and how much the assignment for the current course would be likely to cost.

Sally is uneasy about the discussion and takes various "screenshots" of the discussion. She then approaches the faculty member in charge of the course, Dr. Bell, to discuss what her options are for reporting this. The following conversation takes place:

SALLY:	Some of the students in our class have been using cheating sites. I know of at least Chegg and CourseHero.
DR. BELL:	Thanks for coming forward with this information; how do you know this?
SALLY:	Pat and Jo have been using a cheating site for their assignments in the past and are planning to use it for the first assignment in our course. We formed a study group, and they were talking in our WhatsApp chat about using a cheating site that they have used before.
DR. BELL:	OK, do you have any evidence that could help us prove that this has been happening?
SALLY:	These are the screenshots I have taken of what they said, but if I give you these, they will know that it was me that told the university. There are only the three of us in the WhatsApp group. I don't want any trouble.

Value Discussion

This case study explores the concept of courage through staff and students exploring the relationship between social and moral dimensions of societal interactions. This is explored through a student's desire to exercise their responsibilities as a good member of the academic community and simultaneously preserve their social relationships within their cohort. The issue is further complicated through the potential for negative consequences for a student who is acting as a "whistleblower" within the student body. The relationship of the level of commitment and level of risk for a student in this position is important to this scenario. Staff and students can both consider the nature of courage in relation to contract cheating and the need to balance competing outcomes of courage, responsibility, and privacy.

The value of responsibility is also addressed in the case study as it explores the consequences of personal responsibility. The scenario challenges a student to assess what level of risk they are willing to tolerate to achieve a "moral" outcome. The possibility of social and physical consequences for taking responsibility in a contract cheating situation need to be considered by both the student and the faculty member.

Question Discussion

1. What are the options open to investigate this case?
2. What are the ethical issues with students sharing private correspondence from social media platforms?
3. What methods might the staff member have to investigate a case such as this if Sally is not willing to further share the screenshots with the investigation process?

Conclusion

Whilst acting on reports of misconduct, institutions through their policies, and staff through their actions, have a responsibility to protect the privacy and well-being of those who report this potential misconduct which demonstrates courage.

Case 3: Mock Police Board Exam Puts Students in the Hot Seat

Page C. Spiess, Norwich University, United States

Synopsis/Summary

In Professor Gibson's course students make a presentation and answer a question to replicate the context of a "real" police board. Catherine is a leader in the campus community and takes the exam first. She reveals to seven waiting students the answer to the "secret" question before they enter the exam. Six students never reveal they knew what would be asked ahead of time. Only John, the seventh and final student, admits that he was given the topic prior.

Supporting Information

Professor Gibson's advanced course enables students to experience a "real" police promotion board, which replicates the typical hiring process as a course assignment. Students sit outside of the classroom together. Each student takes their turn entering the classroom, presenting their condensed version of course information, and answering a specific question from Professor Gibson. Students are not aware of the additional question topic ahead of time, as thinking on your feet is part of the assignment itself.

The normal process is that a student would sit down and become an audience member in the classroom after presenting and answering the secret question. However, Catherine presents first because she needs to attend a meeting of campus student leaders. Catherine leaves the classroom, with Professor Gibson's permission, after her turn. In the 30 seconds before Professor Gibson gathers the next student to enter the classroom, Catherine tells her seven waiting classmates "Employment statistics? Really?" Then, Catherine leaves the building to get to her important leadership meeting with university officials. Some of the waiting students look up the employment statistics they had discussed in class, just in case.

Six of the waiting seven students enter the classroom and complete the full assignment, remaining in the classroom afterwards. John, the seventh and final student, enters the room to complete his assignment and states, "Sir, because of the values of this institution, I cannot answer the additional assignment question, even though I know the answer. Catherine told all of us what the question would be when she left the classroom."

Value Discussion

The primary value in this case is courage. Only John, the final student, had the courage to admit that Catherine had revealed the surprise question topic ahead of time. John admitted he could not complete the assignment as requested because he was already told what question Professor Gibson would ask. The fortitude it took to act with high moral character, despite his fear of the consequences, is what demonstrates John acted with courage. Revealing the wrongdoing of a classmate,

Catherine, who was a leader in the campus community, was also a risk that no other student that day was courageous enough to take.

Secondary values found in this case are honesty and fairness. Catherine revealing the topic of the oral exam question to her waiting classmates abolished the impartial nature of the assessment Professor Gibson was attempting to achieve in his assignment. It was unfair of Catherine to taint her classmate's chances at an equitable assessment. Simply by telling her classmates the topic ahead of time, Catherine influenced their ability to be unbiased and answer the exam question in an unprejudiced manner. It is notable that only John, the final student, was honest and revealed he knew what the exam topic was before setting foot in the exam room.

Question Discussion

1. How should Professor Gibson assess each of the seven waiting students' knowledge of the assignment material?
2. What ethical obligations do each of the seven students have towards Professor Gibson, and Catherine, who is a campus community leader in her own right?
3. What ethical obligation does Catherine have to the academic community, and what is the impact of her response when confronted with an academic integrity violation?

Conclusion

The social dynamic within a population significantly affects the student perspective of fairness, with implications regarding views on honesty, and the courage it takes to stand up to peer authority figures.

Case 4: Courage with Coding

Jillian Orfeo, University of Maryland Global Campus, United States

Synopsis/Summary

Jesse is a computer science major with no prior coding experience. The first class is proving challenging. Jesse is falling behind and asks the instructor for help. The professor allows Jesse to redo an assignment without additional guidance. Frustrated, Jesse turns to the internet. The resulting work matches a prior student's submission. When contacted, Jesse acknowledges their actions. A tutoring session is facilitated. Jesse realizes fearing the stigma of needing extra help held them back from using appropriate resources.

Supporting Information

Jesse received a failing grade on the first week's assignment in their coding class. Making things worse, Jesse doesn't understand this week's lesson at all. Jesse sends their instructor an email: "I'm really struggling with the learning material. Can you help me?"

The professor responds, "You don't seem to have a good grasp on the concepts. You can redo the first assignment. Please submit it by Friday."

That gives Jesse two days to figure out what they're doing wrong, and they're working full-time both days. Jesse dives in on their lunch break, but it's hopeless. They're just "too stupid" to get it.

But they're paying for this class, and they've got a promotion on the line—failing the class isn't an option. If they could only look at the solutions to the problems, then they're sure they'll understand it. And if not, there's another whole week until the next assignment is due to learn it. Jesse searches the internet and finds the homework solutions have been posted to a document-sharing website. Grateful, Jesse copies the answers and submits the assignment.

The instructor recognizes the assignment as a prior student's, and emails Jesse: "I gave you the opportunity to redo this assignment. You copied the answers from someone else."

Jesse is flooded with guilt and frustration. Maybe they aren't cut out for computer science. And now they've fallen even further behind. Jesse responds: "I wasn't understanding it, and I didn't have time to figure it out myself."

The professor is faced with a choice: address this as a plagiarism issue or as a failed opportunity to help a struggling student. The professor reluctantly refers the student for tutoring.

The tutoring session opens Jesse's eyes to their own inhibitions that deterred them from seeking appropriate help when they first needed it.

Value Discussion

The primary value of this case study pertains to courage. It takes courage to admit when you need extra help, but also to recognize when someone else does. In this scenario, the student is too embarrassed after being rebuffed by the instructor to ask for yet more help. The student doesn't want anyone else to know they "don't get it." Both the professor and the student could have made different choices initially to get the student the help they needed to be successful moving forward, had they had the courage and understanding to do so.

Question Discussion

1. How might this student have better prepared for taking on this new learning opportunity?
2. What could the instructor have done initially to support this struggling student beyond offering a redo on the assignment?
3. How do faculty build a classroom culture that embraces and anticipates "failures" as part of the learning experience, not just in discipline-specific knowledge and skill development, but also in broader academic skills, such as identifying appropriate sources of help?
4. How do students and institutions address the perceived stigma that prevents some students from seeking appropriate forms of assistance?

Conclusion

The greatest demonstration of courage is both knowing when you need to ask for help and knowing when you can offer someone else additional support to be successful.

Case 5: But I Know This Student Well

Blaire N. Wilson and Jason T. Ciejka , Emory University, United States

Synopsis/Summary

Professor Rodgers has discovered significant plagiarism in an essay submitted in his senior seminar. Kaitlyn has been excellent in her undergraduate career and has even served as a peer tutor and an undergraduate teaching assistant for previous classes taught by Professor Rodgers. Knowing that Kaitlyn has had a difficult semester, Professor Rodgers is reluctant to report the case to the student integrity office. Kaitlyn is applying to graduate programs and working a part-time job on campus, and the academic misconduct process would be yet another stressor.

Supporting Information

Faculty are required to report cases of academic misconduct to the student integrity office (SIO). The SIO reviews and adjudicates all cases of misconduct (both academic and other social or behavioral issues) at the institution. The SIO has both formal and information options for resolving reports of misconduct.

Faculty at the institution complete a mandatory policies and practices training that includes a review of the expectation to report to SIO. The training highlights the importance of reporting cases and illustrates how SIO supports students holistically in their response to issues that arise.

Faculty members in growing numbers have been concerned with the way SIO has handled cases of academic misconduct that are viewed as minor in nature. They fear that the SIO is doling out sanctions that are unreasonable and far too severe. All of this is pure speculation that is growing in various academic departments on campus as faculty have no say in the outcome of cases.

Professor Rodgers wrote several letters of recommendation for Kaitlyn for graduate school and in a few cases sent personal emails to his colleagues at those institutions citing Kaitlyn's strong academic performance in his courses. Professor Rodgers even submitted Kaitlyn for a departmental award that is given to two outstanding seniors who show great promise.

Professor Rodgers is aware that Kaitlyn has recently begun working a part-time job on campus in response to an unexpected financial challenge in her family. Kaitlyn is unable to rely on her family as much as she had expected, and the part-time job keeps the rent paid and the lights on at her off-campus apartment.

Value Discussion

The primary value in this case is courage. Concerns that a decision may be unpopular or might create an uncomfortable situation often stem from fear—fear that the decision may have an adverse impact on a relationship or fear that the decision will be unwelcomed or met with anger or great disappointment. Difficult decisions, therefore, require courage from the decision maker. Courage is the commitment to one's values and ethics despite any perceived repercussions.

Responsibility is one of the secondary values in this case. At most institutions, faculty have a duty to address or report cases of academic misconduct. This is a responsibility laid upon them by the institution both to protect the value of academic integrity and to provide due process and consistency for students suspected of misconduct. Shirking the responsibility to report misconduct and prioritizing an established relationship with a student contributes to possible inequity in the process and potential favoritism.

Another secondary value is respect. Professor Rodgers has an opportunity to show his respect for the academic misconduct process and the SIO by reporting the case. Professor Rodgers can also demonstrate respect for Kaitlyn by alerting her to the issue, encouraging her through the process, and finding ways to support her elsewhere in the course. Reminding Kaitlyn that he has a duty to report the case, but that he also wants to see her succeed in the remainder of the course would remind Kaitlyn that she can overcome this obstacle.

Question Discussion

1. How can Professor Rodgers follow the process, but also demonstrate that he supports Kaitlyn as a student and cares about her success and well-being?
2. What are the potential risks if Professor Rodgers does not report the incident and tries to handle it on his own?
3. Are there ways the faculty could have supported the student earlier in the semester that would have led to a better outcome?

Conclusion

Though it can be difficult and it takes courage for faculty to report students with whom they have a close relationship, faculty have a responsibility to follow the established process in their institutions.

Case 6: To Pursue or Not Pursue

Kaela Lindquist and Sharisse Stafford, University of North Carolina at Charlotte, United States

Synopsis/Summary

Julia is a graduate faculty member in the department of computer science. Julia realized that several students collaborated on the final exam without permission and submitted code that was nearly identical. Julia wants to hold the students accountable but is struggling because several students are international, and an unsatisfactory grade will result in removal from the program and visa cancellation. The program director is also concerned about the number of students who would be dismissed if they receive unsatisfactory grades.

Supporting Information

Julia sets up a meeting with each of the students to discuss her concerns. During her meeting with Joseph, she learns he organized several study sessions with his classmates and created a group chat where people actively shared ideas and files related to the final. He added, "I knew several of my classmates were struggling, and I just wanted to help them." Joseph also shared his education is being sponsored by his home country and he has one semester left before he graduates. If he is removed from the program, he does not have the ability to repay the sponsorship.

Another student, Maria, shared that the students have worked together in the past. She said, "You never said anything about our previous assignments, so we thought it was okay." Julia decided to review past assignments, and realized several students submitted similar work with the midterm. Julia reviewed her syllabus language, which clearly stated students could not collaborate on the final. After talking to the students, Julia determines 20 out of 25 violated policies.

Julia reaches out to the program director to get advice on how to proceed with holding the students accountable. The program director tells her, "We are under a lot of pressure to retain students and boost our graduation rates. If you fail all the students, it is going to create a lot of problems." Julia learns the students must receive a C or better or they will be academically suspended. The program director asks Julia to "just give them a warning." Julia does not believe a warning is enough, but she does not want the students to be suspended.

After careful consideration, Julia decides to reduce their course grades by one letter grade. This results in the students who collaborated earning a C in the course.

Value Discussion

The primary fundamental value for this case study is courage. Despite pressure from the program director and knowing some students may face additional financial or visa related issues, Julia felt strongly that a warning would not properly address her concerns. Instead, Julia displays courage by issuing a consequence that she felt addressed the severity of the behavior even though it may impact student retention.

Fairness is a secondary value presented in this case study. Julia displays fairness by inviting the students to meet with her so she could better understand what occurred. She listened to their individual circumstances and was able to take that information into account when she was determining an appropriate consequence. She also clearly stated her expectations in the course syllabus. She considered how the consequence could impact domestic and international students differently and issued a consequence that could be applied to both demographics without a disproportionate impact.

Responsibility is also a value presented in this case study. Julia displays responsibility to her students by sharing her concerns with them and pointing out how their behavior was against the expectations listed in the syllabus. She also recognized this situation overlapped with other policies or program needs and sought advice from the program director before she issued a consequence for the violation of policy, which showed responsibility to the institution, faculty peers, and administrators. She showed responsibility to herself by weighing several factors as she considered the appropriate outcome and issuing a consequence that allowed for the students to be held accountable for their actions while also giving them an opportunity to continue their education.

Question Discussion

1. As a faculty member, what other options does Julia have for addressing the violation of policy?
2. In what ways can Julia be consistent and fair, while also taking into consideration individual circumstances?
3. What other policies or departments may be impacted by a proposed consequence?
4. What role does the administration play in addressing Julia's concerns and supporting the students?

Conclusion

Although a consequence may have a disproportionate impact on students, having the courage to address academic misconduct is essential to upholding the integrity of a program.

Case 7: The Handy Dandy Dictionary

Christian Moriarty, St. Petersburg College, United States

Synopsis/Summary

A paper from one of Professor Miranda Alenko's students, Jack Arterius, is turned in with strange language. While none of it is technically grammatically incorrect, it reads like a computer learned English yesterday without ever understanding what an idiom is. No noun is ever used twice, and any that may be fit to be used again has an incompatible synonym shoe-horned in. The similarity checker report shows some reproduced results from outside sources, but from multiple places and papers and nothing definitive.

Supporting Information

Miranda Alenko, a psychology professor, assigned her students a research paper on psychological ailments of their choice, going over its history, first diagnoses, and current understanding in the literature.

Professor Alenko received a paper from an otherwise good student, Jack Arterius, that seemed unusual. Nothing in the paper is exactly wrong, per se, but the grammar and language feels off. Looking at it for a while, she notices that no noun that has a synonym is used twice. The word "mania" is used in the beginning (a psychological term), but every subsequent reference to the concept uses a different word, such as "crazy," then "insane," then "crazed," then "hysteria." This happens with both psychological terms and non-psychology terms, and most of the words are not appropriate in context and feel like someone using a thesaurus too zealously.

The language is unusual, too, in that it is tangentially English, but feels like a computer learning it as a second language. It sort of makes sense if you squint, but no one who has learned English, first language or not, would write this way. Everything is stilted and idiomatic language is used like an alien has come from Mars trying to fit in.

When a similarity checker is run on the paper, it highlights commonish phrases here and there in the middle of sentences, but nothing comes back definitively. When compared to Jack's previous papers in the course, his older writing seems much more normal.

Value Discussion

The primary fundamental value for this case study is courage. Students must have the courage to make choices that are ethically right but may land them not getting a paper in on time or not passing a class. If something is due soon or a student doesn't understand a concept and is scared of failing, plagiarizing and using an auto-thesaurus is not just cheating, but it's cheating themselves out of an education. Faculty, too, must have the courage to have uncomfortable conversations with students on potential cheating when there isn't definitive proof of it.

The second fundamental value for this case study is honesty. Students must be honest when they write papers, and that includes being honest in that everything turned in with their name attached is their own, original writing. Using an auto-thesaurus on a lifted or contracted paper is not original work, and it is dishonest to claim otherwise. While honest writing can feel more difficult at first, it becomes second-nature over time to write in your own voice. That's the point of education, after all!

Question Discussion

1. As a faculty member, how can you fairly determine whether the student is indeed plagiarizing or cheating?
2. How can faculty approach the student and discuss this cheating practice?
3. How can faculty and integrity offices educate students on reducing the incidence of this cheating strategy and encourage courage and honesty in writing assignments?

Conclusion

While some students have learned that they can put contracted or plagiarized papers through auto-thesaurus programs changing as many words as possible to synonyms, students must have the courage to be honest in their education.

Case 8: The Blackmail Blues

Greg Preston, University of Newcastle, Australia

Synopsis/Summary

A student approaches the academic integrity office at their university. They inform the office that they used an essay mill service for two assignments in their first year of study. They are now being blackmailed by the essay mill who are demanding additional payments to ensure that the university doesn't find out about their previous conduct.

Supporting Information

A first-year student, Sam, was very stressed about the assignments for their Introduction to History survey course. They saw a number of online ads for a contract cheating site, Assignmenthelp4you. They employed that assignment mill to prepare the two written assignments for their course and paid $70 for each assignment. Sam passed that course by submitting the work prepared by the contract cheating site as if it was their own work. Twelve months later Assignmenthelp4you contacted Sam via email and told them that they knew that the work they had sold to them was submitted to their university, and unless Sam paid them an additional $200 they would inform the university that the work had been purchased from their site.

Sam has outlined the basics of the case to the university's integrity office and requested a meeting. At that meeting the following conversation takes place:

SAM: I have made a big mistake and I don't know what to do.

INTEGRITY OFFICER: Tell me about it.

SAM: I know it was wrong, but I bought two assignments in the first year and the people that I bought them from want more money. I don't have any money to pay them, and I am worried about what will happen with my studies. How can I make this right?

Value Discussion

The case study explores the concept of courage through staff and students investigating the relationship between past behaviors and the consequences of that behavior. Further there is the opportunity to consider the development of character and the transient nature of both character and reputation. Both staff and students can consider the nature of courage in relation to contract cheating and the need for courage to balance competing actions based on moral outcomes.

This case study also explores the development of honesty through complex situations. It highlights ways that "teachable moments" can be maximized to develop honesty in students. Further it demonstrates that in key moments, staff can display the importance of truth in the resolution of issues. It will allow staff and students to explore some differing motivations for honesty as the basis of lifelong integrity.

Question Discussion

1. What options are open to the academic integrity officer to deal with this case?
2. Should blackmail cases be treated differently than other cases of "self-disclosure" of previous misconduct?

Conclusion

Students and faculty are facing increasingly complex moral decisions in relation to contract cheating involving blackmail situations with increasing courage being required to navigate multifaceted situations.

Case 9: Taking a Stand for Integrity: A Whistleblower's Tale

Shiva Sivasubramaniam, University of Derby, United Kingdom

Synopsis/Summary

Saxena noticed two different academics (one from her institution), though friends and working in the same field, never tried to collaborate with each other. Then she found out that they were using each other as reviewers for their papers to receive favorable decisions. Saxena has reported this to retraction watch (with evidence), who have made this public, which has resulted in their manuscripts being retracted by many journal editors. She then started receiving hate emails from them; the internal researcher also indirectly hindered her academic progression.

Supporting Information

Dr. Saxena Ahmed has been working in a well-reputed university for the past five years. She collaborates with her colleague Prof. Adam Johnston, an internationally renowned scientist in the field of neurobiology. She has been introduced to Dr. Jane Brathwaite, another reputed scientist in this field working in another research institute, by Prof. Johnston. She also found out that Adam and Jane have been close friends since their university days and have been working in the same field for the past 15 years. However, they never collaborated with each other. She enquired about this to Adam's senior technician Mr. Ram Kumar. He jokingly replied "Well, they are purposely not collaborating to use each other as reviewers for their papers to receive favorable decisions and speedy publications."

Astonished by this, Saxena carried out a search on their submission histories which confirmed Ram's claim. She then collected those evidence and reported this misconduct to retraction watch, who have made this public. Subsequently both Adam's and Jane's manuscripts have been retracted by many journal editors. Saxena then started receiving hate emails from Adam and Jane; Adam indirectly hindered her academic progression too. Additionally, she faced institutional pressures which has led her to move to another university.

Value Discussion

This case study emphasizes the importance of courage, as a primary value, to identify and report professional misconduct without worrying about repercussions. In this scenario, a junior academic detects the misconduct of a professor, she collates evidence to prove this alleged fraudulent misbehavior and reports it to an external body (retraction watch) whilst protecting the initial source. Even though her collaborator and his accomplice are internationally renowned scientists, she was not afraid to whistle-blow their professional misconduct. Since her manager is in a higher position and has the power to determine her research directions of that institution, she faced professional repercussions. Yet she was brave enough and had the courage to uphold integrity without worrying about the consequences. Young and upcoming authors like Saxena should have the courage to report any questionable research/publication practices.

Being honest is one of the important ethical principles that should be abided by everyone and is one of the secondary values in this case study. A properly carried out blind peer review ensures high standards by publishing validated and original findings/innovations. Yet, despite being researchers in the medical profession, Prof. Johnston and Dr. Braithwaite have been dishonest and systematically planned and carried out professional misconduct for a long time. This would have not only tarnished the trustworthiness of their research outputs but also resulted in serious health implications to the public. This dishonest behavior engenders validity and scientific irreproducibility. It also disputes medical research. Unfortunately, this type of peer review manipulation is becoming increasingly and worryingly common. Several scientists are still engaged in these kinds of fraudulent activities which should have been reported by whistleblowers such as Saxena.

Responsibility and being accountable for every action in research is another secondary value in this case study. Whether they are authors, reviewers, publishers, or even a new researcher/academic, they have the responsibility to behave ethically. When reporting scientific findings in a form of publication, authors have a responsibility to not only truthfully report the results without manipulation but also to recommend the names of neutral experts in the field to review their submission by critically assessing the importance, novelty, and the impact of the paper submitted. Many journals are encouraging the authors to provide the names of suitable reviewers with the expectation that authors show responsibility and professionalism to choose an impartial expert. In this scenario both Prof. Johnston and Dr. Braithwaite failed to abide by this. On the other hand, Saxena, has shown her responsibility as a fellow scientist to report this activity to stop this fraudulent behavior.

Fairness is the final secondary value addressed in this case study. The main aim of peer review is establishing and assuring the quality of the data/findings that are to be published. Therefore, the process should be impartial, critical, but fair by being supportive to improve the quality. This can only be established by a neutral reviewer whose decisions should not be influenced by mutual benefits. The unethical collaboration between Prof. Johnston and Dr. Braithwaite to produce favorable publication decisions is not fair to other researchers who undergo neutral and impartial reviews of their publications. In addition, this behavior is not fair to other scientists and/or the public who would have trusted the findings by the two researchers and followed up investigation or abided by what had been reported by them. Moreover, when their questionable publication practices were exposed by Saxena, they both unfairly treated her.

Question Discussion

1. As a responsible scientist, what additional measures could Saxena have taken before contacting retraction watch?
2. Discuss any proactive institutional or other measures that can be applied to enhance honesty and maintain fairness?
3. Discuss the ways to motivate people to have the courage to "speak up" or report questionable behavior?

Conclusion

Everyone should have the courage to report the fraudulent behavior of people misusing their fame and power to protect research integrity and the community from the effects of unethical professional practices.

Case 10: Demonstrating Courage to Stand for Integrity

Shiva Sivasubramaniam, University of Derby, United Kingdom

Synopsis/Summary

Frank was excited about submitting his first scientific manuscript as a senior/corresponding author. He submitted the paper for internal review for feedback. After about a week, the head of research (HoR), wanted to have a meeting with Frank. During this meeting, the HoR commended his work, then he said it has everything a paper should have except one, the HoR's name is missing! He continued that putting his name as co-senior author would increase the chances of his paper being accepted.

Supporting Information

Dr. Frank Illingworth is a newly appointed lecturer in a reputed university, he attained his position after a three-year post-doctoral position in a different institution. His university has an internal policy that all manuscripts and grant applications should first undergo an internal review process to ascertain high standards. He submitted his manuscript via the internal research portal suggesting two internal reviewers.

After about two weeks Frank received a call from Ms. Marie Daiken, the executive secretary to the head of research (HoR) Prof. Trip Dixon, asking him for a meeting with the professor. Frank excitedly shouted, "My first paper as senior author has gained the attention of the HoR!" He met Trip after two days, it was a friendly meeting in which Trip started by saying, "I have read your excellent paper, I have no doubt it will get published." He further said, "You know what? Your research directions fit very well with my strategic research theme! I think we should collaborate." Frank got excited and started explaining his research aspirations. After about 30 minutes of what looked like a meaningful discussion, Trip said, "Well young man, I will surely support your paper being submitted for publication, it has everything a paper should have except one important thing, my name is missing!" and continued, putting his name as co-senior author, would increase the chances of his paper being accepted. Despite this, Frank submitted without Trip's name as he never contributed to this study.

Value Discussion

This case study emphasizes the importance of courage, as the primary value, to ignore managerial pressures and abide by integrity principles. In this scenario, a junior academic is being indirectly allured and/or intimidated to include his manager's name in a publication to which the latter never contributed. Since his manager is in the highest position and has the power to determine the research directions of that institution, non-compliance with his request might affect the junior academic's career. Despite this, the lecturer had the courage to ignore this unfair and unethical demand and submitted the paper without giving any credit to the HoR.

Fairness is a secondary value presented in this case study. Being fair with transparency is an important ethical expectation in academia, research, or everything we do. In this scenario, a junior academic was indirectly expected to include the HoR's name in a research publication without any contributions from the latter to the project. In other words, the HoR's position was used to take unfair advantage. This type of practice, though not uncommon, jeopardizes the institutional and individual reputation and sets a bad example for the profession. Institutions and individuals should work together to prevent people from gaining unfair advantages. This needs institutional policy, governance, and staff education.

Responsibility is also a value presented in this case study. Responsible behavior is one of the pillars of research ethics that should be abided by everyone. The senior managers such as research professors should set a particular example for being and acting responsibly. They should not abuse their position to obtain "gift authorships" without significant contributions to the study. Unfortunately, several junior researchers are being pressured to provide gift authorship to their senior managers and their collaborators. In this case, the HoR almost directly demanded this. On the other hand, the junior researcher has the responsibility to resist such expectations and if necessary, report to the internal ethical governance committee.

Question Discussion

1. What responsible measures should an institution employ to minimize these types of intimidations?

2. What other responsible measures could Frank, as a professional researcher, have taken within his institution before submitting the paper?
3. Considering there aren't any institutional measures to safeguard victims (such as Frank), what do you think the consequences will be of Frank submitting his paper without giving gift authorship to his HoR?
4. What other measures could Frank have taken, outside his institution to safeguard himself from future repercussions?

Conclusion

It is important to have the courage to face up to the misuse of power to unfairly demand unethical practices by superiors, who should be role models for good behavior. Speaking up and resisting unfair demands requires courage.

Case 11: Self-Plagiarism in PhD Student's Thesis

Tatjana Odineca and Ilze Birzniece, Riga Technical University, Latvia

Synopsis/Summary

Professor Kalnbergs, a respected member of the scientific community, develops his second PhD thesis. During the check, the plagiarism detection tool shows the compilation of almost fully copy-pasted parts of published papers and research where Prof. Kalnbergs was one of the co-authors. All sources are mentioned in the bibliography, although sometimes they are not cited in the body of his thesis. Neither his supervisor nor commission members pay attention to that fact as they are not willing to doubt the academic integrity of a colleague. Prof. Kalnbergs successfully presents his thesis.

Supporting Information

When questioned, Prof. Kalnbergs stated: "I agree that there must be some strict rules like mentioning the sources in the bibliography or putting the references. Integrity in academic writing is important but paraphrasing my own published research is just ridiculous. To be sure, I was not the only or even the first author of those research and papers but I'm still the co-author, so I can say these were MY research papers!"

Next, his supervisor adds, "Most PhD students use their published papers and research for the thesis. Not copy/paste, of course, paraphrasing is obligatory and self-citing shouldn't be that long . . . but Prof. Kalnbergs is an elderly man who is not too familiar with these formalities."

The other commission members add "I am not sure how big Kalnbergs' personal contribution was in that research and papers he used for the thesis . . . but he was mentioned as a co-author, so formally everything is OK. Self-plagiarism is not such a big sin as real plagiarism. Why should we pick on his thesis? He's a well-known and respected professional. I worked with him on many projects. He deserves to get one more PhD degree at the end of his career."

Value Discussion

The primary fundamental value for this case study is courage. The supervisor did not point out Prof. Kalnbergs' mistakes and turned a blind eye for fear of hurting the feelings of a respected colleague. Though the commission members were not sure if Prof. Kalnsbergs' contribution to the research was significant, they accepted the thesis without comments, because of fear of questioning the academic integrity and professional-ism of their colleague. Academic staff must have the courage to treat all students equally, apply the same requirements to all works they check, and not make exceptions based on their personal attitudes.

A secondary fundamental value for this case study is honesty. Aca-demic honesty means "compliance with ethical and professional princi-ples, standards, practices, and consistent system of values, which serves as guidance for making decisions and taking actions in education, research, and scholarship" (Tauginienė et al., 2018). It is unknown how significant Prof. Kalnbergs' contribution to the published materials where he was mentioned as a co-author was and which he used for his thesis. From the words of the committee member (who seems to be informed), it can be concluded that the contribution was not that big and the credit for co-authors should be emphasized in the thesis. It was against ethical and professional principles, and unfair towards other authors to use the materials without any change. Honest behavior includes responsibility for the outcome and impression made by your work.

The third fundamental value for this case study is responsibility. Kalnbergs does not take the term "self-plagiarism" seriously and does not see the problem in his thesis. The responsibility of Prof. Kalnbergs, both as a student and a member of the scientific community, is to know and respect the principles of academic integrity and to act according to these principles. The responsibility of the supervisor is to point out the student's mistakes, including violation of the rules of academic writing and academic integrity. Both supervisor and commission members share responsibility for accepting suspicious or low-quality PhD theses and awarding degrees to their developers, without engaging in unpleasant discussion of the actual contribution of the PhD aspirant.

Question Discussion

1. How should the supervisor address the situation with courage?
2. What is the responsibility of the commission in such cases?
3. To what extent are honesty and trust endangered in this case?

Conclusion

Neither supervisor nor commission members pay significant attention to self-plagiarism in a well-known professor's PhD thesis, not willing to doubt the academic integrity of a respected colleague. It takes courage to raise the questions in a situation where personal interests and employment relationships are involved.

Reference

Tauginienė, L., Gaižauskaitė, I., Glendinning, I., Kravjar, J., Ojsteršek, M., Ribeiro, L., Odiņeca, T., Marino, F., Cosentino, M., Sivasubramaniam, S., and Foltýnek, T. *Glossary for Academic Integrity*. ENAI Report 3G [online]: revised version, October 2018.

Appendix A
Alphabetical List of Case Studies Mapped to the Fundamental Values

P-Primary Value; S-Secondary Value

Case Study Title	Trust	Honesty	Fairness	Respect	Responsibility	Courage
A Syllabus Sleight of Hand		P			S	S
Abuse of Power by Medical Teachers: Can We Still Become Role Models?				S	P	
Advising Not Policing: Respecting the Students			S	P		
All for One and One for All		S	P		S	
Alma Mater Should Always Matter		S			P	
But I Know This Student Well				S	S	P
But They'll Never Know	P	S		S		
Buyers' Remorse		P			S	S
Can't Put My Finger on It			P	S	S	
Capturing the Impostor Syndrome Through Turnitin	P	S		S		
Caught in the Act		P			S	
Clear as . . . Mud	P		S			
Collusion by Coercion			P		S	
Collusion Confusion		S	P		S	
Contract Cheating Coercion		S			P	
Courage with Coding		S				P

182

Case						
Demonstrating Courage to Stand for Integrity			S		S	P
Does Co-Authorship Imply a Responsibility for the Whole Document?		S	S		P	P
Don't Harm the Messenger					S	S
Email Déjà Vu		S		P	S	S
Fake Grade Booster Classes			S		P	S
Flagrant Foul on the Faculty			P		S	S
Foiling Attempts to Facilitate File Sharing: Updating Assessments		P			S	
Higher Learning, Higher Stakes		S	P		S	S
Investment Pains		P	P		S	
It Doesn't Add Up			P		P	
It's Not My Problem Until It's Been Turned In			P		P	S
Machine Learning: Trusting the Training Data, or the Trainer?	P	S			S	S
Mock Police Board Exam Puts Students in the Hot Seat		S	S		P	P

(Continued)

(Continued)

Case Study Title	Trust	Honesty	Fairness	Respect	Responsibility	Courage
Multi-use Presentations, "Retritos"			P		S	S
My Students, My Research Subjects—Trust in Faculty, Researcher, and Student Relationships	P	S		S	S	S
One Size Fits All					P	
Personalized and Supportive Proctoring Processes	S		S	P		
Photoshop: The Easiest (Worst!) Way Out	S	P		S		S
Posting Faulty Information to Bait Students		S			P	
Pressure vs. Courage: The Dean's Dilemma	P		S			S
Procedural Empathy			P	S		
Professor Purposely Publishes Student Paper Without Giving Credit		P			S	
Punishment and Rehabilitation			S	P		
Readied Recalcitrance		P	S		S	

184

Reduce, Reuse, Recycle	P	S			
Respect and Honor Through Intentional Proactive Student Actions	S	S	P		
Scaffolding Writing for an A	S	S	S	P	
Self-Plagiarism in PhD Student's Thesis				S	P
Should I Pay the Contract Cheating Sites to Get the Answer?	P	S		S	
Socialize with Specialists to Spot and Stem Spinning		P		S	
Statistically Surprising Standardized State-Wide Scores Sold		S		P	
Student's Legal Defense and Institutional Responsibility	S	S		P	
Suspicious Success	S	S		S	
Taking a Stand for Integrity: A Whistleblower's Tale	S	S		S	P
Telling Family Secrets	P	S		S	

(Continued)

(Continued)

Case Study Title	Trust	Honesty	Fairness	Respect	Responsibility	Courage
That's Not Fair: Balancing the Workload for Remote Teams	S		S		P	
The Blackmail Blues		S				P
The Emotional Rollercoaster of Reporting			S	P		
The Handy Dandy Dictionary		S				
Time Is a Non-Renewable Resource		S		P	S	P
Tipping the Scale: Mental Health and Outcomes			S	P		
To Burn Bridges or to Build Them?		P				
To Pursue or Not Pursue			S		S	P
To Tell or Not to Tell: That Is the Question		S			S	P
Towards Fair and Balanced Budgeting			P	S		
Using Relational Coordination to Promote Academic Integrity	P		S	S	S	
Weighing the Options			S		P	

186

Title				
What Do You Mean Students Are In Charge?	P		S	S
When the Bones Are Good: Laying the Foundation for Faculty	S		P	S
Where in the Metaverse Is Boris' Voice?	P	S	S	
Where's Waldo: IP Address Incongruence and Student Surrogacy		P		

Appendix B
Alphabetical List of Case Studies Mapped to Audience

P-Primary Audience; S-Secondary Audience

Case Study Title	Students	Faculty	Academic Integrity Office	Researcher	Admin.
A Syllabus Sleight of Hand	S	P			S
Abuse of Power by Medical Teachers: Can We Still Become Role Models?	S	P			
Advising Not Policing: Respecting the Students	S		P		
All for One and One for All	P	S			
Alma Mater Should Always Matter		P			
But I Know This Student Well	S	P			
But They'll Never Know	P				
Buyers' Remorse	P	S			
Can't Put My Finger on It	S	P	S		
Capturing the Impostor Syndrome Through Turnitin	S	P			
Caught in the Act		S			P
Clear as . . . Mud	P	S			
Collusion by Coercion	P	S			S
Collusion Confusion		P			
Contract Cheating Coercion	S		P		S
Courage with Coding	P	S			

190

Demonstrating Courage to Stand for Integrity		S		P	S
Does Co-Authorship Imply a Responsibility for the Whole Document?		P	S		
Don't Harm the Messenger	P	S			
Email Déjà Vu		P			S
Fake Grade Booster Classes	S	P			
Flagrant Foul on the Faculty	S	P			S
Foiling Attempts to Facilitate File Sharing: Updating Assessments		P	S		
Higher Learning, Higher Stakes	P				
Investment Pains	P	S	S		
It Doesn't Add Up		S			
It's Not My Problem Until It's Been Turned In	P	S		P	
Machine Learning: Trusting the Training Data, or the Trainer?	P	S			

191

(Continued)

Case Study Title	Students	Faculty	Academic Integrity Office	Researcher	Admin.
Mock Police Board Exam Puts Students in the Hot Seat	P				
Multi-use Presentations, "Retritos"	S	P			
My Students, My Research Subjects—Trust in Faculty, Researcher, and Student Relationships	S	P			
One Size Fits All	S	P			
Personalized and Supportive Proctoring Processes	S		P		
Photoshop: The Easiest (Worst!) Way Out	P				S
Posting Faulty Information to Bait Students		P			
Pressure vs. Courage: The Dean's Dilemma		S			P; S-staff
Procedural Empathy	S	P			
Professor Purposely Publishes Student Paper Without Giving Credit	P				S

Punishment and Rehabilitation	S	S	P
Readied Recalcitrance	S	P	
Reduce, Reuse, Recycle	P	S	
Respect and Honor Through Intentional Proactive Student Actions	P	S	
Scaffolding Writing for an	P		S
Self-Plagiarism in PhD Student's Thesis	S	S	P
Should I Pay the Contract Cheating Sites to Get the Answer?		P	S
Socialize with Specialists to Spot and Stem Spinning	S	S	P-authenticity team S
Statistically Surprising Standardized State-Wide Scores Sold	P	S	
Student's Legal Defense and Institutional Responsibility			P
Suspicious Success	S	P	S

193

(Continued)

(Continued)

Case Study Title	Students	Faculty	Academic Integrity Office	Researcher	Admin.
Taking a Stand for Integrity: A Whistleblower's Tale			S	P	
Telling Family Secrets	S		P		
That's Not Fair: Balancing the Workload for Remote Teams	S	P			
The Blackmail Blues		S	P		
The Emotional Rollercoaster of Reporting		P	S		
The Handy Dandy Dictionary		P			
Time Is a Non-Renewable Resource	S	P			
Tipping the Scale: Mental Health and Outcomes			P		S
To Burn Bridges or to Build Them?					P
To Pursue or Not Pursue	S	P	S		
To Tell or Not to Tell: That Is the Question	P	S			

194

Towards Fair and Balanced Budgeting			P	S
Using Relational Coordination to Promote Academic Integrity			P	S
Weighing the Options	P	S		
What Do You Mean Students Are in Charge?		S	P	S
When the Bones Are Good: Laying the Foundation for Faculty		P	S	
Where in the Metaverse Is Boris' Voice?		P		S; S-librarian
Where's Waldo: IP Address Incongruence and Student Surrogacy	S	P		

Appendix C
Case Studies by Author

Author	Title
Akin, I.	*That's Not Fair: Balancing the Workload for Remote Teams*
Akpan, E.I.	*Scaffolding Writing for an A* *Capturing the Impostor Syndrome Through Turnitin*
Armyanti, I.	*Abuse of Power by Medical Teachers: Can We Still Become Role Models?*
Asroruddin, M.	*Abuse of Power by Medical Teacher: Can We Still Become Role Models?*
Birzniece, I.	*Self-Plagiarism in PhD Student's Thesis*
Blake, V.	*Where in the Metaverse Is Boris' Voice*
Bollenback, D.	*Where's Waldo: IP Address Incongruence and Student Surrogacy*

(Continued)

(Continued)

Author	Title
Bourgoin, J.	*Advising Not Policing: Respecting the Students* *Procedural Empathy* *Tipping the Scale: Mental Health and Outcomes* *When the Bones Are Good: Laying the* *Foundation for Faculty*
Ciejka, J.T.	*A Syllabus Sleight of Hand* *Alma Mater Should Always Matter* *But I Know This Student Well* *But They'll Never Know* *Email Déjà Vu* *Flagrant Foul on the Faculty* *It's Not My Problem Until It's Been Turned In* *Pressure vs. Courage: The Dean's Dilemma* *Time Is a Non-Renewable Resource* *To Burn Bridges or to Build Them?* *What Do You Mean Students Are in Charge?*
Clark, A.	*Collusion by Coercion*
Claybrooks, G.	*That's Not Fair: Balancing the Workload for* *Remote Teams*
Collett, D.	*Where in the Metaverse Is Boris' Voice*
Cruz, L.M.P.	*Photoshop: The Easiest (Worst!) Way Out*
Cullen, C.	*Collusion Confusion*

Currie, E.	*Advising Not Policing: Respecting the Students*
	Procedural Empathy
	Tipping the Scale: Mental Health and
	   Outcomes
	When the Bones Are Good: Laying the
	   Foundation for Faculty

(Continued)

Author	Title
Daumiller, M.	*Fake Grade Booster Classes*
	Professor Purposely Publishes Student Paper Without Giving Credit
	My Students, My Research Subjects—Trust in Faculty, Researcher, and Student Relationships
Denney, V.P.	*Baiting the Offender*
Escalón, D.A.C.	*Photoshop: The Easiest (Worst!) Way Out*
Facciolo, L.	*The Emotional Rollercoaster of Reporting*
Frank, K.	*Socialize with Specialists to Spot and Stem Spinning*
Frankovitch, L.	*Buyers' Remorse*
Frase, H.	*Socialize with Specialists to Spot and Stem Spinning*
Fritz, T.	*My Students, My Research Subjects—Trust in Faculty, Researcher, and Student Relationships*
Glassman, A.	*Where's Waldo: IP Address Incongruence and Student Surrogacy*
Kellogg, S.	*Clear as . . . Mud*
	Don't Harm the Messenger
	Higher Learning, Higher Stakes
	Investment Pains
	One Size Fits All
	Reduce, Reuse, Recycle
	Suspicious Success
	Weighing the Options

(Continued)

(Continued)

Author	Title
Kennedy, P.	*Does Co-Authorship Imply a Responsibility for the Whole Document?* *Punishment and Rehabilitation*
Kunov, H.	*Does Co-Authorship Imply a Responsibility for the Whole Document?* *Punishment and Rehabilitation*
Lentz, C.	*Where's Waldo: IP Address Incongruence and Student Surrogacy*
Liang, A.	*Should I Pay the Contract Cheating Sites to Get the Answer?*
Lindquist, K.	*To Pursue or Not Pursue*
Mayo, C.E.P.	*Can't Put My Finger on It* *It Doesn't Add Up* *Telling Family Secrets*
Mazarakis, A.	*Where in the Metaverse Is Boris' Voice*
McDermott, B.	*Socialize with Specialists to Spot and Stem Spinning*
McEdwards, T.	*Caught in the Act*
Moriarty, C.	*Contract Cheating Coercion* *Readied Recalcitrance* *Statistically Surprising Standardized State-Wide Scores Sold* *Student's Legal Defense and Institutional Responsibility* *The Handy Dandy Dictionary*

(Continued)

or	Title
phy, G.	*Towards Fair and Balanced Budgeting*
rien, M.	*Personalized and Supportive Proctoring Processes*
Odineca, T.	*Self-Plagiarism in PhD Student's Thesis*
Orfeo, J.	*Courage with Coding*
Orta-Anes, E.	*Multi-Use Presentations, "Refritos"*
Spiess, P.C.	*Mock Police Board Exam Puts Students in the Hot Seat*
Palombi, D.	*The Emotional Rollercoaster of Reporting*
Pavlova, I.	*The Emotional Rollercoaster of Reporting*
Pfeiffer, A.	*Socialize with Specialists to Spot and Stem Spinning*
Pittsenberger, C.	*Personalized and Supportive Proctoring Processes*
Ponce, E.	*The Emotional Rollercoaster of Reporting*
Preston, G.	*All for One and One for All* *The Blackmail Blues* *To Tell or Not to Tell: That Is the Question*
Price, O.M.	*Foiling Attempts to Facilitate File Sharing: Updating Assessment*
Pringle, P.	*Respect and Honor Through Intentional Proactive Student Actions*

(Continued)

(Continued)

Author	Title
Rahimian, M.	*Using Relational Coordination to Promote Academic Integrity*
Redquest, E.	*The Emotional Rollercoaster of Reporting*
Rogerson, A.M.	*Foiling Attempts to Facilitate File Sharing: Updating Assessment*
Salazar, D.G.	*Photoshop: The Easiest (Worst!) Way Out*
Sivasubramania, S.	*Demonstrating Courage to Stand for Integrity* *Taking a Stand for Integrity: A Whistleblower's Tale*
Sledge, S.	*Respect and Honor Through Intentional Proactive Student Actions*
Spiess, P.	*Mock Police Board Exam Puts Students in the Hot Seat*
Stafford, S.	*To Pursue or Not Pursue*
Tejoyuwono, A.A.T.	*Abuse of Power by Medical Teachers: Can We Still Become Role Models?*
Thacker, E.J.	*Collusion by Coercion*
Vargas, K.	*Socialize with Specialists to Spot and Stem Spinning*
Wills, M.S.	*Machine Learning: Trusting the Training Data, or the Trainer*

(Continued)

r	Title
n, B.N.	*A Syllabus Sleight of Hand*
	Alma Mater Should Always Matter
	But I Know This Student Well
	But They'll Never Know
	Email Déjà Vu
	Flagrant Foul on the Faculty
	It's Not My Problem Until It's Been Turned In
	Pressure vs. Courage: The Dean's Dilemma
	Time Is a Non-Renewable Resource
	To Burn Bridges or to Build Them?
	What Do You Mean Students Are in Charge?
Wolf, J.	*Advising Not Policing: Respecting the Students*
	Procedural Empathy
	Tipping the Scale: Mental Health and Outcomes
	When the Bones Are Good: Laying the Foundation for Faculty

Appendix D
Case Studies by Country of Origin

Country of Origin	Title	Author(s)	Institution(s)
Australia	*All for One and One for All*	Preston, G.	University of Newcastle
	Foiling Attempts to Facilitate File Sharing: Updating Assessment	Rogerson, A.M. Price, O.M.	University of Wollongong
	The Blackmail Blues	Preston, G.	University of Newcastle
	To Tell or Not to Tell: That Is the Question	Preston, G.	University of Newcastle
Canada	*Collusion by Coercion*	Thacker, E.J. Clark, A.	University of Toronto York University
	Does Co-Authorship Imply a Responsibility for the Whole Document?	Kennedy, P. Kunov, H.	University of Toronto
	Punishment and Rehabilitation	Kennedy, P. Kunov, H.	University of Toronto
	Should I Pay the Contract Cheating Sites to Get the Answer?	Liang, A.	University of Saskatchewan
	The Emotional Rollercoaster of Reporting	Facciolo, L. Redquest, E. Ponce, E. Pavlova, I.	McMaster University Sheridan College

	Title	Authors	University
	Using Relational Coordination to Promote Academic Integrity	Palombi, D. Rahimian, M.	Huron at Western University
Germany	*Fake Grade Booster Classes My Students, My Research Subject—Trust in Faculty, Researcher, and Student Relationships*	Daumiller, M. Fritz. T. Daumiller. M.	University of Augsburg University of Augsburg
	Professor Purposely Publishes Student Paper Without Giving Credit	Daumiller, M.	University of Augsburg
Indonesia	*Abuse of Power by Medical Teachers: Can We Still Become Role Models?*	Armyanti, I. Tejoyuwono, A.A.T Asroruddin, M.	Universitas Tanjungpura. Pontianak
Latvia	*Self-Plagiarism in PhD Student's Thesis*	Odineca, T. Birzniece, I.	Riga Technical University

(Continued)

Country of Origin	Title	Author(s)	Institution(s)
México	*Photoshop: The Easiest (Worst!) Way Out*	Cruz, L.M.P. Escalón, D.A.C. Salazar, D.G.	Tecnológico de Monterrey
Nigeria	*Capturing the Impostor Syndrome Through Turnitin*	Akpan, E.I.	American University of Nigeria
	Scaffolding Writing for an A	Akpan, E.I.	American University of Nigeria
Puerto Rico	*Multi-Use Presentations, "Refritos"*	Orta-Anes, E. Mendez, A.G.	Universidad Ana G. Mendez-Recinto de Gurabo
Switzerland	*Where in the Metaverse Is Boris' Voice*	Blake, V.	EF Academy, United States
		Collett, D. Mazarakis, A.	Independent Consultant International School Basel

United Kingdom	*Demonstrating Courage to Stand for Integrity*	Sivasubramaniam, S.	University ⌐
	Taking a Stand for Integrity: A Whistleblower's Tale	Sivasubramaniam, S.	University of Derby
United States	*A Syllabus Sleight of Hand*	Ciejka, J.T.	Emory University
		Wilson, B.N.	
	Advising Not Policing: Respecting the Students	Currie, E.	Vanderbilt University
		Wolf, J.	
		Bourgoin, J.	
	Alma Mater Should Always Matter	Wilson, B.N.	Emory University
		Ciejka, J.T.	
	Baiting the Offender	Denney, V.P.	Embry-Riddle Aeronautical University
	But I Know This Student Well	Wilson, B.N.	Emory University
		Ciejka, J.T.	
	But They'll Never Know	Wilson, B.N.	Emory University
		Ciejka, J.T.	
	Buyers' Remorse	Frankovitch, L.	University at Buffalo
	Can't Put My Finger on It	Mayo, C.E.P.	Quinnipiac University
	Caught in the Act	McEdwards, T.	Oregon State University
	Clear as . . . Mud	Kellogg, S.	Iowa State University

(Continued)

209

(Continued)

Country of Origin	Title	Author(s)	Institution(s)
	Collusion Confusion	Cullen, C.	University of Georgia
	Contract Cheating Coercion	Moriarty, C.	St. Petersburg College
	Courage with Coding	Orfeo, J.	University of Maryland
	Don't Harm the Messenger	Kellogg, S.	Iowa State University
	Email Déjà Vu	Ciejka, J.T. Wilson, B.N.	Emory University
	Flagrant Foul on the Faculty	Wilson, B.N. Ciejka, J.T.	Emory University
	Higher Learning, Higher Stakes	Kellogg, S.	Iowa State University
	Investment Pains	Kellogg, S.	Iowa State University
	It Doesn't Add Up	Mayo, C.E.P.	Quinnipiac University
	It's Not My Problem Until It's Been Turned In	Ciejka, J.T. Wilson, B.N.	Emory University

Machine Learning: Trusting the Training Data, or the Trainer	Wills, M.S.	Embry-Riddle cal University
Mock Police Board Exam Puts Students in the Hot Seat	Spiess, P.C.	Norwich University
One Size Fits All	Kellogg, S.	Iowa State University
Personalized and Supportive Proctoring Processes	Pittsenberger, C. O'Brien, M.	Western Governors University
Pressure vs. Courage: The Dean's Dilemma	Ciejka, J.T. Wilson, B.N.	Emory University
Procedural Empathy	Currie, E. Wolf, J. Bourgoin, J.	Vanderbilt University
Readied Recalcitrance	Moriarty, C.	St. Petersburg College
Reduce, Reuse, Recycle	Kellogg, S.	Iowa State University
Respect and Honor Through Intentional Proactive Student Actions	Sledge, S.	Christopher Newport University
	Pringle, P.	Norfolk State University

(Continued)

Country of Origin	Title	Author(s)	Institution(s)
	Socialize with Specialists to Spot and Stem Spinning	Pfeiffer, A. Frase, H. Frank, K. McDermott, B. Vargas, K.	Western Governors University
	Statistically Surprising Standardized State-Wide Scores Sold	Moriarty, C.	St. Petersburg College
	Student's Legal Defense and Institutional Responsibility	Moriarty, C.	St. Petersburg College
	Suspicious Success	Kellogg, S.	Iowa State University
	Telling Family Secrets	Mayo, C.E.P.	Quinnipiac University
	That's Not Fair: Balancing the Workload for Remote Teams	Akin, I. Claybrooks, G.	American College of Education
	The Handy Dandy Dictionary	Moriarty, C.	St. Petersburg College
	Time Is a Non-Renewable Resource	Wilson, B.N. Ciejka, J.T.	Emory Universi⁺

Title	Authors	Institution
Tipping the Scale: Mental Health and Outcomes	Currie, E. Wolf, J. Bourgoin, J.	Vanderbilt U...
To Burn Bridges or to Build Them?	Wilson, B.N. Ciejka, J.T.	Emory University
To Pursue or Not Pursue	Lindquist, K. Stafford, S.	University of North Carolina at Charlotte
Towards Fair and Balanced Budgeting	Murphy, G.	University of Rochester
Weighing the Options	Kellogg, S.	Iowa State University
What Do You Mean Students Are in Charge?	Ciejka, J.T. Wilson, B.N.	Emory University
When the Bones Are Good: Laying the Foundation for Faculty	Currie, E. Wolf, J. Bourgoin, J.	Vanderbilt University
Where's Waldo: IP Address Incongruence and Student Surrogacy	Glassman, A. Lentz, C. Bollenback, D.	Embry-Riddle Aeronautical University

Index

A

Abuse of Power by Medical Teachers: Can We Still Become Role Models?, 143–146
Adjudication:
  of breach of confidentiality, 61–63
  budget for, 92–94
Advising not Policing: Respecting the Students, 121–122
Advisors:
  and borrowing of calculator, 81–82
  on fair reporting, 93
  unconscious bias of, 121–122
Akin, Imani, 146–148
Akpan, Emilienne Idorenyin, 50–53, 127–129
All for One and One for All, 71–73
Alma Mater Should Always Matter, 139–141
Alumni, 61–63, 139–141
Anonymous accusation, 150–152
Armyanti, Ita, 143–146
Article, not crediting student's work in, 9–11
Artificial intelligence, 36–43
Ashamed student, 114–115
Asroruddin, Muhammad, 143–146

Assessments:
  impartial nature of, 162
  online-proctored, 118–120
  of student efforts, 50
  survey about cheating on, 56–58
  updating, 24–26
Assignment mill, 159, 171–172
Athletes, special treatment for, 90–92
Authenticity:
  in academic work, 23
  and artificial intelligence, 36–38
  and spinning, 95–97
  verifying, 120

B

Baiting the Offender, 132–133
Banking, machine learning in, 39
Bias, 53, 68, 121–122. *See also* Fairness
Birzniece, Ilze, 178–180
Blackmail:
  for contract cheating, 150–152
  by essay mill, 171–173
The Blackmail Blues, 171–173
Blake, Vivienne, 36
Bollenback, Denise, 18–24

215

Boosting grades, classes for, 141–143
Borrowing:
    of calculator, 81–83
    of peer's laptop, 7–9
Bourgoin, Jeremy, 88–90, 111–113, 116–118, 121–122
Budget:
    fairness of, 92–94
    student project related to, 47
Bullying, 74
Business, machine learning in, 39–43
But I Know this Student Well, 164–166
But They'll Never Know, 46–48
Buyers' Remorse, 5–7

C
Calculator, 81–83
Camera:
    obscene gesture on, 84–86
    with online proctoring, 119
Campus:
    culture of, 93
    modeling community values of, 30
Can't Put My Finger On It, 84–86
Capturing the Impostor Syndrome through Turnitin, 50–53
Caught in the Act, 26–29
Center for teaching, 110
Chat, *see* Group chat
Chegg, 159
Chemistry lab reports, 43–44
Ciejka, Jason T., 29–32, 46–48, 53–55, 63–65, 75–77, 90–92, 107–111, 139–141, 164–166
Citation. *See also* Plagiarism
    and artificial intelligence, 36–38
    in drafts, 77–79
    missing, 91
    and procedural empathy, 88–90
City planning, 47
Claybrooks, Gail, 146–148
Clear as . . . Mud, 43–44
Cliff Notes, 38
Code of conduct, 84
Code of ethics, 114
Coding:
    stigma of asking for help with, 162–164
    unauthorized collaboration on, 167–169

Coercion:
    collusion by, 73–74
    to pay contract cheating company, 150–152
Cole, Sally, vii
Collaboration. *See also* Group chat
    with campus partners, 29–30
    for cheating on exams, 107–109
    with chemistry lab partners, 43–44
    cross-department, 95–97
    with plagiarizing, 138
    to promote academic integrity, 60
    on remote teams, 147
    unauthorized, 14–26
    in upholding integrity, 94
    without permission, 167–169
Collett, David, 36
Collusion:
    in cheating ring, 130–132
    penalty for, 73–75
    on take-home exams, 79–81
Collusion by Coercion, 73–75
Collusion Confusion, 79–81
Computer science, 162–164, 167–169
Confidentiality:
    of academic integrity processes, 55
    breach of, 61–63
Confronting misconduct, 58, 77, 162
Consent, 41
Contract cheating:
    assignment mills, 159, 171–172
    essay mills, 171–173
    with online proctoring, 26–29
    payment for, 14–16, 150–152
Contract Cheating Coercion, 150–152
Copying. *See also* Plagiarism
    in chemistry lab reports, 43–44
    of coding answers, 162–164
    detection of, 37
Courage, xi, 153–180
    The Blackmail Blues, 171–173
    But I Know this Student Well, 164–166
    case studies focused on faculty/academic integrity office, 155
    case studies focused on researchers, 155–156
    case studies focused on students, 154–155

2225Index5555

e with Coding, 162–164
strating Courage to Stand for Integrity, 176–178
Harm the Messenger, 156–158
ness secondary to, 70
e Handy Dandy Dictionary, 169–171
honesty secondary to, 4
Mock Police Board Exam Puts Students in the Hot Seat, 160–162
To Pursue or Not Pursue, 167–169
respect secondary to, 102
responsibility secondary to, 128
as secondary value, 6–7, 13, 32, 55, 58, 88, 156
Self-plagiarism in PhD Student's Thesis, 178–180
Taking a Stand for Integrity: A Whistle-blower's Tale, 173–175
To Tell or Not to Tell: That is the Question, 158–160
Courage with Coding, 162–164
Coursehero, 159
Crediting work, 2
of co-authors, 178–180
for staffing solution, 29–30
of student, publishing without, 9–11
Critical thinking, 38, 51
Cruz, Lucila María Puente, 11–14
Cullen, Courtney, 79–81
Culture:
of faculty reporting, 113
of honesty, 2, 30, 104
of integrity, 55, 58, 80, 81, 154
integrity aspect of, 93
Currie, Elaine, 88–90, 111–113, 116–118, 121–122

D
Data analysis:
with machine learning, 39–43
of online exam answers, 80
Daumiller, Martin, 9–11, 56–58, 141–143
Dean(s):
on budget requests, 92–94
and sanction for public official's daughter, 53–55
Deception. *See also* Honesty
changing grade with Photoshop, 11–14

research and learning free from, 38
as slippery slope, 133
with syllabus design, 31–32
Demonstrating Courage to Stand for Integrity, 176–178
Denney, Valerie P., 132
Dictionary, 128, 169–171
Discretion. *See also* Flexibility
in applying sanctions, 53–55
with non-academic conduct, 86
when student tests boundaries, 50
Does Co-Authorship Imply a Responsibility for the Whole Document?, 137–139
Don't Harm the Messenger, 156–158

E
Email Déjà Vu, 109–111
Embarrassment, in asking for help, 164
The Emotional Rollercoaster of Reporting, 105–107
Empathy, 88–90, 100, 117
Escalón, Dulce Abril Castro, 11–14
Essays:
and artificial intelligence, 36–38
grades on vs. learning process with, 127–129
plagiarism in, 164–166
Essay mill, 171–173
Ethics:
activities encouraging ethical behavior, 102–105
of attorneys, 150
in co-authorship, 138
code of, 114
commitment to fairness, 91–92
for crediting co-authors, 178–180
expectations for ethical environment, 37
and pressure to name co-author, 177
promoting unethical behavior, 52
in reporting cheating incident, 109
in reviewing papers, 173–175
Evidence. *See also* Screenshots
in culture of honesty, 2
from group chat, 108
of integrity of student work, 49
for student cheating, 8
of student surrogacy, 19–23
unconscious bias based on, 121–122

Exams. *See also* Tests
  accusation of cheating on, 63–65
  collaboration for cheating on, 107–109
  contract cheating sites, 11–14
  Googling questions on, 116–118
  police board, mock, 160–162
  practice, for licensing, 130–132
  proctoring vendors, 26–29
  sanctions for cheating on, 53–55
  take-home, collusion on, 79–81
  unauthorized collaboration on, 167–169
Expectations:
  about systems, 41
  adjusted for budget level, 94
  clear statement of, 87, 168
  for community members, 92
  for ethical environment, 37
  for faculty reporting, 113
  faculty responsibility for following, 32
  fair implementation of, 50
  of fairness, 68
  in grade booster classes, 141–143
  in literacy program, 129–129
  in promoting trust, 34
  for reporting cases, 165
  of students, stating, 15
  for work of graduate students, 77–79
Extension, denial of request for, 48–50, 76

F
Facciolo, Laura, 105–107
Failing:
  changing grade on transcript, 11–14
  of gateway course, 108
  of international students, 167–169
  stigma of asking for help when, 162–164
Fairness, ix–x, 67–97
  All for One and One for All, 71–73
  Can't Put My Finger On It, 84–86
  case studies focused on academic
      integrity office and authentic-
      ity team, 69
  case studies focused on faculty/adminis-
      trators, 68–69
  case studies focused on students, 68
  Collusion by Coercion, 73–75
  Collusion Confusion, 79–81

courage secondary to, 156
  Flagrant Foul on the Faculty, 90
  Higher Learning, Higher Stakes,
  honesty secondary to, 4
  It Doesn't Add Up, 81–83
  *It's Not My Problem Until It's Been
      Turned In,* 75–77
  Multi-use presentations, "Refritos," 86–8
  Procedural Empathy, 88–90
  of remote team workload, 146–148
  respect secondary to, 102
  responsibility secondary to, 126
  as secondary value, 15, 17, 44, 50, 55,
      59–60, 62, 65, 70, 106, 115, 118,
      120–122, 128–129, 131, 136,
      138–139, 142–143, 147, 149–150,
      162, 168, 175, 177
  *Socialize with Specialists to Spot and Stem
      Spinning,* 95–97
  Towards Fair and Balanced Budgeting,
      92–94
Fake Grade Booster Classes, 141–143
FERPA, 62
File-sharing sites, 24–26
Flagrant Foul on the Faculty, 90–92
Flexibility. *See also* Discretion
  based on student life experiences,
      118–120
  in sanctions, 116–118
*Foiling Attempts to Facilitate File Sharing:
      Updating Assessment,* 24–26
Frank, Katie, 95–97
Frankovitch, Loretta, 5–7
Frase, Heather, 95–97
Fraud:
  machine learning for detecting, 39–43
  research and learning free from, 38
  in reviewing papers, 173–175
Fritz, Tanja, 56–58
Fundamental values, vii–xi. *See also
      individual values*
Fundamental Values of Academic
      Integrity, 13

G
Game, academic offenses as a, 114–116
Gesture, obscene, 84–86

Aaron, 18–24
nce, to prevent unfair
 advantage, 177
GPA. *See also* Failing
ected by survey answers, 56–58
fter unauthorized collaboration, 168
changing failing grade, 11–14
GPA booster classes, 141–143
for international student, 105–107
learning process vs., 127–129
and obscene gesture on camera, 84–86
for public official's daughter, 53–55
on reused work, 45–46
Graduate student:
 expectations for work of, 77–79
 not crediting work of, 9–11
 professional experience for, 30
Group chat, 59
 in cheating on exam, 108
 for circumventing procedures, 158–160
 for coding final, 167–169
 sharing information through, 156–158
Group projects:
 faculty fairness in handling, 90–92
 plagiarism by one member, 71–77
 responsibility with co-authorship,
  137–139
 reuse of presentations for, 86–88
 similar reports for, 43–44
 trust in, 46–48
Guidelines:
 to avoid misconduct, 128
 student responsibility to follow, 108
 working within, 43–44

H
The Handy Dandy Dictionary, 169–171
Hearing boards, faculty on, 63–65
Help websites, 79–81, 132–135, 162–164
Higher Learning, Higher Stakes, 77–79
High school, transition to college from, 51
History, 71–73
Homework:
 online assignment purchase, 5–7
 similar submissions, 7–9
 student responsibility in, 87
 suspicion of misconduct with, 135–137

Honesty, viii–ix, 1–32
 To Burn Bridges or To Build Them?, 29–30
 Buyers' Remorse, 5–7
 case studies focused on faculty/adminis-
  trators, 2–3
 case studies focused on students, 2
 Caught in the Act, 26–29
 courage secondary to, 156
 culture of, 2, 30, 104
 fairness secondary to, 70
 in feedback, 100
 Foiling Attempts to Facilitate File Sharing:
  Updating Assessment, 24–26
 Investment Pains, 7–9
 Photoshop: The Easiest (Worst!) Way
  Out, 11–14
 Professor Purposely Publishes Student
  Paper Without Giving Credit, 9–11
 Readied Recalcitrance, 16–18
 respect secondary to, 102
 responsibility secondary to, 126
 as secondary value, 4, 38, 48, 50, 52, 72,
  78, 81, 104, 109, 111, 115, 133,
  138–139, 141, 150, 152, 162, 170,
  172, 174, 179–180
 Should I Pay the Contract Cheating Sites
  to Get the Answer?, 14–16
 A Syllabus Sleight of Hand, 31–32
 trust secondary to, 36
 Where's Waldo: IP Address Incongruence
  and Student Surrogacy, 18–24
Honor code, 51, 91, 103
Honor Council:
 student-governed, 63–65
 value of joining, 102–105
Human development, 49
Humiliation, 73

I
Impartiality. *See also* Fairness
 of assessments, 162
 ideal of, 142–143
 in reviewing papers, 175
 in treating students, 55, 87, 88, 91–92
Integrity:
 academic, 13–15, 59–61, 92 (*See also*
  specific topics)

Integrity: *(Continued)*
    culture of, 55, 58, 80, 81, 154
    of degrees and documentation, 14
    expectations for, 34
    honesty as core of, 2, 15, 27 (*See also* Honesty)
    modeling, 15–16, 111
    promoting, 25
    of student work, 46
    systems, 41
    upholding values of, 28, 124
Integrity offices, 8, 9, 94, 165
Intellectual property, 137
Intent:
    in conducting survey, 57
    in proactive student actions, 102–105
    in sanctioning process, 89
International students:
    changing of failing grade by, 11–14
    fellowship application, 139–141
    pressure not to fail, 167–169
    reporting suspected plagiarism by, 105–107
Intimidation, into academic misconduct, 73–74
Investment Pains, 7–9
IP addresses, 18–24, 80
It Doesn't Add Up, 81–83
It's Not My Problem Until It's Been Turned In, 75–77

J
Journal reviewers, 173–175

K
Kellogg, Sara, 7–9, 43–46, 48–50, 77–79, 134–137, 156–158
Kennedy, Pamela, 114–116, 137–139
Kunov, Hans, 114–116, 137–139

L
Lab:
    chemistry lab reports, 43–44
    falsifying data from, 121–122
Language proficiency, 105–107, 127–129
Late work, request for extension on, 48–50
Laws:
    awareness of, 39
    legal defense of processes, 126, 148–150

Lentz, Cheryl, 18–24
Liability, FERPA, 62
Liang, Ann, 14–16
Liberal arts, 50–53, 127
Librarian, 36–38
Lindquist, Kaela, 167–169
Literacy program, 127–129

M
McDermott, Ben, 95–97
McEdwards, Tay, 26–29
Machine learning, 39–43
Machine Learning: Trusting the Training Data, or the Trainer, 39–43
Manipulation, 41, 174–175
Manuscript:
    naming co-author on, 176–178
    retraction of, 173–175
Math:
    calculus, 156–158
    quantitative reasoning, 31–32
Mayo, Claude E. P., 61–63, 81–86
Mazarakis, Alexa, 36
Medical professionals:
    abuse of power by, 143–146
    professional misconduct by, 173–175
Mendez-Recinto de Gurabo, Ana G., 86–88
Mental health, 116–118
Metaverse, 36–38
Methods:
    for circumventing procedures, 158–160
    not taught in class, 14–16
Misconduct. *See also specific types of misconduct*
    changing grade on transcript, 11–14
    in chemistry lab reports, 43–44
    duty to report, 92, 166
    integrity office handling of, 165
    intimidation into, 73–74
    not being found responsible for, 63–65
    paying for proof of, 14–16
    policy on, 128–129
    by public official's daughter, 53–55
    retaliation for reporting, 158–160
    reusing previous work, 45–46
    of reviewers, 173–175
    rules/policies for handling, 16
    student reporting of, 156–158

's denial of, 7–9, 16–18,
      ↓3–44, 134
   ⌐ion of, 135–137
   to identify, 51
   'olice Board Exam Puts Students in the
      Hot Seat, 160–162
⌐eling:
   by faculty and administrators, 111,
      142, 143, 145
   of fairness, 68
   of good behavior, 133
   honesty, 2, 11, 15, 16
   integrity, 15–16
   machine learning in, 39–43
   as medical teacher, 145
   by medical teachers, 143–146
   responsibility, 25, 28, 124
   values of campus community, 30
Money laundering, 39–43
Moral compass, 114
Moral decisions, 172, 173
Moral dimension of social dynam-
      ics, 159–161
Moriarty, Christian, 16–18, 130–132,
      148–152, 169–171
Multi-use presentations, "Refritos," 86–88
Murphy, Greer, 92–94
My Students, My Research Subjects—Trust
      in Faculty, Researcher and Student
      Relationships, 56–58

O
Objectivity:
   attitude of, 104
   for effective learning process, 88
   in enforcing policies, 136–137
   in evaluating student work, 50
O'Brien, Maureen, 118–120
Odineca, Tatjana, 178–180
Ombudsperson, 73–74
One Size Fits All, 134–135
Open-note exam, 69
Oral exam, 160–162
Orfeo, Jillian, 162–164
Organized contract cheating, 26–29
Originality:
   and the metaverse, 36–38
   paper-sharing site, 16–18

and spinning, 95–97
student surrogacy, 18–24
using paper from previous course,
      45–46
Orta-Anes, Edna, 86–88

P
Palombi, Danielle, 105–107
Pavlova, Iryna, 105–107
Payment:
   for contract cheating, 14–16, 150–152
   to essay mill, 171–173
   for licensing test answers, 130–132
   for online assignments, 5–7
   for proof of misconduct, 11–14
Penalty. See also Sanctions
   for collusion, 73–74
   for a group member's plagiarism, 71–73
   for reusing work, 45–46
   and student's mental health, 116–118
   for using help website, 134–135
Personalized and Supportive Proctoring
      Process, 118–120
Pfeiffer, Abby, 95–97
Philosophy, 45–46
Photoshop: The Easiest (Worst!) Way
      Out, 11–14
Pittsenberger, Carissa, 118–120
Plagiarism:
   alerting professor to, 103
   and artificial intelligence, 36–38
   auto-thesaurus use, 169–171
   draft paper without citations, 77–79
   in email message, 109–111
   inconsistent treatment of, 90–92
   by international student, 105–107
   by one group member, 71–77
   with paper-sharing site, 16–18
   and procedural empathy, 88–90
   research and learning free from, 38
   responsibility with co-
      authorship, 137–139
   reusing work, 45–46
   self-, in thesis, 178–180
   by stressed undergraduate, 164–166
   by synonym replacement, 155
Police board exam, 160–162
Policing, advising vs., 121–122

Policies:
    for academic integrity, 15
    accountability with, 96
    breaking promise to follow, 5–7
    for contract cheating, 28
    convincing stakeholders to go
        beyond, 58–61
    demonstrating regard for, 50
    equitable enforcement of, 136–137
    exceptions to, 76–77
    fairness of, 68
    for handling misconduct, 16
    and honesty, 2
    individualized outcomes vs., 116–118
    of integrity, 55
    for internal review, 176–178
    knowing and following, 124
    letter vs. spirit of, 83
    in literacy program, 129–129
    mandatory training in, 165
    and obscene gesture on camera, 84
    to prevent unfair advantage, 177
    for remote team work, 147
    respect for, 74
    on reuse of work, 86–88
    on unauthorized assistance, 82, 168
    for writing and assignments, 23
Political science, 46–48
Ponce, Enrique, 105–107
Presentations:
    plagiarism by one group member, 71–73
    reused, 86–88
Pressure:
    to apply sanctions, 53–55
    in foreign study, 12
    to name co-author, 176–178
    resisting, 53
    to retain students, 167
    on whistleblower, 174
*Pressure vs. Courage: The Dean's
    Dilemma,* 53–55
Preston, Greg, 71–73, 158–160, 171–173
Price, Oriana Milani, 24–26
Pringle, Pam, 102–105
Privacy:
    of academic integrity processes, 55, 149
    of whistleblowers, 159, 160
Proactive student actions, 102–105
Procedural Empathy, 88–90

Procedures:
    circumventing, 158–160
    to enforce rules, 87–90
    fairness of, 68, 88–90
    for handling misconduct, 16
    and honesty, 2
    individualized outcomes vs., 116–118
Process(es):
    of academic integrity, 61–63, 92, 118–12
    within group work, 72
    investigative, 89–90, 111–113, 121–
        122, 148–150
    legal defense of, 126, 148–150
    for misconduct referrals, 135
    for proctoring, 118–120
    in student-governed honor system, 63–65
Proctoring:
    by online vendor, 26–29
    process for, 118–120
    and test anxiety, 118–120
*Professor Purposely Publishes Student Paper
    Without Giving Credit,* 9–11
Proofreading, 75–77
Protections:
    for faculty and students, 85
    legal, 137
Psychology, 169–171
Public official, sanction for daughter
    of, 53–55
Publishing:
    journal reviewers, 173–175
    pressure to name co-author, 176–178
    without crediting student, 9–11
Punishment and Rehabilitation, 114–116

Q
Question Formulation Technique
    (QFT), 41–43
Quiz:
    sharing information about, 156–158
    similar answers on, 134–135
Quotation, 91

R
Rahimian, Matt, 58–61
Readied Recalcitrance, 16–18
Redquest, Eluze, 105–107
Reduce, Reuse, Recycle, 45–46

ns, 13

ation, focus on, 114–116

al coordination, 58–61

nships:

ong reviewers, 173–175

nd duty to report misconduct, 164–166

personal, confidentiality and, 61–63

and plagiarized email, 110

respect in, 129

social, 159

between staff and reporting faculty, 113

teacher-student, 56–58

Reliability of systems, 41

Remote teams, balancing workload
for, 146–148

Reprisals/repercussions, see Retaliation/
reprisal/repercussion

Reputation:

and breach of confidentiality, 61–63

and collusion, 74

conflicts threating to harm, 48

of institutions, 141

and pressure to name co-author, 177

Resolution:

making decisions for, 147

trust in finding, 63, 146

truth in finding, 172

Respect, x, 99–122

Advising not Policing: Respecting the
Students, 121–122

case studies focused on academic integrity office and office of community
standards, 101

case studies focused on faculty/adminis-
trators, 100–101

case studies focused on students, 100

Email Déjà Vu, 109–111

The Emotional Rollercoaster of Reporting, 105–107

fairness secondary to, 70

honesty secondary to, 4

Personalized and Supportive Proctoring
Process, 118–120

Punishment and Rehabilitation, 114–116

Respect and Honor through Intentional
Proactive Student Actions, 102–105

responsibility secondary to, 128

as secondary value, 13, 38, 48, 52, 57, 60,
89–90, 94, 101–102, 129, 145, 166

Time is a Non-Renewable Resource,
107–109

Tipping the Scale: Mental Health and
Outcomes, 116–118

trust secondary to, 36

When the Bones are Good: Laying the
Foundation for Faculty, 111–113

Respect and Honor through Intentional Proactive Student Actions, 102–105

Responsibility, x–xi, 123–152

Abuse of Power by Medical Teachers:
Can We Still Become Role Models?, 143–146

Alma Mater Should Always Matter,
139–141

Baiting the Offender, 132–133

case studies focused on academic
integrity office and administration, 125–126

case studies focused on faculty, 124–125

case studies focused on students, 124

Contract Cheating Coercion, 150–152

Does Co-Authorship Imply a Responsibility for the Whole Document?,
137–139

fairness secondary to, 70

Fake Grade Booster Classes, 141–143

honesty secondary to, 4

One Size Fits All, 134–135

respect secondary to, 102

Scaffolding Writing for an Assignment,
127–129

as secondary value, 6, 9, 11, 15–16, 18,
25, 28, 32, 50, 52–53, 57, 60, 65, 72,
74, 78, 80–81, 83, 85, 87–88, 92, 96,
108, 110–111, 113, 126–127, 157,
160, 166, 168, 174–175, 177, 180

Statistically Surprising Standardized
State-wide Scores Sold, 130–132

Student's Legal Defense and Institutional
Responsibility, 148–150

That's Not Fair: Balancing the Workload
for Remote Teams, 146–148

trust secondary to, 36

Weighing the Options, 135–137

Restoration:

of faith after special treatment, 91–92

of integrity, 81

of respect, 110

Restoration (*Continued*)
of self-esteem and confidence, 114
of trust, 54–55
Resubmitting/redoing/correcting assignments:
following plagiarism, 90–92
of groups, 75–77, 90–92
for partial credit, 136
unauthorized help with, 163
Retaliation/reprisal/repercussion:
for reporting misconduct, 74, 158–160
for sharing quiz answers, 157
for survey answers, fear of, 56–58
for unfounded suspicions, 9
for whistleblower, 173–175
Retraction, 173–175
Reviewers:
of group project, 86–88
of international fellowship application, 139–141
for possible spinning, 95–97
in remote work, 146–148
whistleblower on, 173–175
Rogerson, Ann M., 24–26
Rules:
for academic integrity, 13, 15
accountability with, 96
breaking promise to follow, 5–7
for contract cheating, 28, 152
fairness of, 68
institutional/governmental, 145
knowing and following, 124
procedures to enforce, 87

S
Safety of information, 42
Sanctions. *See also* Penalty
for academic dishonesty, 51
for cheating, 17
for collusion on online exams, 80
by integrity office, 165
intention factor in, 89
for not paying tutor bill, 5–7
for plagiarism by international student, 105–107
for plagiarism in group project, 137–139
for public official's daughter, 53–55

Scaffold, honesty as, 10–11
Scaffolding Writing for an Assignme[nt], 127–129
Science:
honesty in, 10–11
reviewers of papers in, 173–175
Screenshots:
of cheating ring, 130–132
of contract cheating, 151, 152
of group chat, 157
of using assignment mills, 158–160
Self-plagiarism in PhD Student's Thesis, 178–180
Senate, 36, 63–65
Sharing. *See also* Group chat
answers to practice tests, 130–132, 160–162
as confidentiality breach, 61–63
file-sharing sites, 24–26
during investigative process, 89–90
paper-sharing website, 16–18
of quiz information, 156–158
of remote team responsibility, 147
on survey answers, 56–58
websites for, 59
Should I Pay the Contract Cheating Sites to Get the Answer?, 14–16
Similarity:
captured by Turnitin, 50–53
of group project reports, 43–44
paper-sharing website, 16–18
in psychology paper, 169–171
of student papers, 71–73
Sivasubramaniam, Shiva, 173–178
Sledge, Sally, 102–105
Socialize with Specialists to Spot and Stem Spinning, 95–97
Social media, 140
Social media groups, 59, 158–159
Spiess, Page C., 160–162
Spinning, 95–97
Stafford, Sharisse, 167–169
Stakeholders:
in academic integrity policy, 65
confidence in abilities of, 52
investment in academic integrity initiatives by, 58–61

demic writing, 18
creditation, 32
tation, 89, 90
sequences for infringing, 13
urage in upholding, 157
designing syllabus to meet, 31–32
for fairness, 83
and grade booster classes, 141–143
for syllabus design, 31–32
for writing and assignments, 23
Statistically Surprising Standardized State-wide Scores Sold, 130–132
Stigma, of asking for help, 162–164
Struggle/struggling:
    with anxiety, 136
    with coding, 162–164
    of international students, 167
    with language proficiency, 105–106
    with organization, 47
    probing questions about, 119
    on science exam, 82
Students. *See also* International students
    assumptions made about, 121–122
    confidence of, 51
    demonstrating honesty to, 15
    different IP addresses for, 18–24
    fear of survey answers by, 56–58
    honor system governed by, 63–65
    inconsistent treatment of, 90–92
    intentional proactive actions of, 102–105
    legal defense for, 148–150
    not crediting work of, 9–11
    obscene gesture made by, 84–86
    respecting ideas of, 100
    respecting life experiences of, 118–120
    syllabus design for attracting, 31–32
Student conduct. *See also* Misconduct
    cheating, 7–9
    chemistry lab reports, 43–44
    draft paper without citations, 77–79
Student council, 56
Student integrity office, 28, 165
Student's Legal Defense and Institutional Responsibility, 148–150
Student surrogacy:
    contract cheating, 26–29
    IP address differences with, 18–24

Survey:
    about honor and integrity, 103
    on extent of cheating, 56–58
Suspicious Success, 48–50
Syllabus:
    deception in designing, 31–32
    for GPA booster class, 142
    guidance within, 44
    statement of expectations in, 87, 168
A Syllabus Sleight of Hand, 31–32
Systems integrity, 41

T
Take-home exam, 69
Taking a Stand for Integrity: A Whistle-blower's Tale, 173–175
Technology. *See also* Tools
    artificial intelligence, 36–38
    auto-thesaurus, 169–171
    machine learning, 39–43
    online proctoring and test anxiety, 118–120
Tejoyuwono, Agustina Arundina Trihardja, 143–146
Telling Family Secrets, 61–63
Tests. *See also* Exams
    proctoring, 26–29
    student offered copy of, 103, 104
Test anxiety, 118–120
Text-matching, 71–73
Thacker, Emma J., 73–75
That's Not Fair: Balancing the Workload for Remote Teams, 146–148
Thesaurus, 169–171
Thesis, self-plagiarism in, 178–180
Third parties:
    online proctoring vendors, 26–29
    test answer sites, 79–81
Threat. *See also* Blackmail
    to out student for contract cheating, 150–152
    to whistleblower, 173–175
Time is a Non-Renewable Resource, 107–109
Tipping the Scale: Mental Health and Outcomes, 116–118
To Burn Bridges or To Build Them?, 29–30

226

INDEX

Tools:
  artificial intelligence, 36–38
  for cheating, 59
  citation, 91
  to identify misconduct, 51
  for plagiarism detection, 178–180
To Pursue or Not Pursue, 167–169
*To Tell or Not to Tell: That is the
  Question*, 158–160
*Towards Fair and Balanced
  Budgeting*, 92–94
Transparency:
  about cheating, 131
  in decision-making, 54
  as ethical expectation, 177
  and GPA booster classes, 142–143
  in group project, 47–48
  with long-term plans, 124
  not acting with, 13
  of policies, 68, 76–77
  setting expectations for, 37
  in survey research, 57
  of systems, 41
  in team building, 147
  and trust, 34, 47, 64
Trust, ix, 33–65
  But They'll Never Know, 46–48
  *Capturing the Impostor Syndrome
    through Turnitin*, 50–53
  case studies focused on academic
    integrity office, 35–36
  case studies focused on faculty/adminis-
    trators, 35
  case studies focused on students, 34–35
  Clear as. . . Mud, 43–44
  courage secondary to, 156
  fairness secondary to, 70
  honesty secondary to, 4
  *Machine Learning: Trusting the Training
    Data, or the Trainer*, 39–43
  *My Students, My Research Subjects—
    Trust in Faculty, Researcher and
    Student Relationships*, 56–58
  *Pressure vs. Courage: The Dean's
    Dilemma*, 53–55
  Reduce, Reuse, Recycle, 45–46
  respect secondary to, 102

  responsibility secondary to, 126
  as secondary value, 13, 36, 113,
    142–143, 147
  Suspicious Success, 48–50
  Telling Family Secrets, 61–63
  as two-way interaction, 100
  *Using Relational Coordination to Prom
    Academic Integrity*, 58–61
  *What Do You Mean Students are in
    Charge?*, 63–65
  *Where in the Metaverse is Boris'
    Voice*, 36–38
Turnitin, 45, 50–53
Tutor:
  for coding student, 163
  on contract cheating site, 14–16
  for online exams, 79–81
  unpaid bill from, 5–7

U
Unauthorized assistance:
  and borrowed calculator, 81–83
  with coding exam, 167–169
  from contract cheating site, 14–16
  help websites, 79–81, 132–135, 162–164
  remorse for, 114–116
  student legal defense against, 148–150
  study-resource sites, 132–133
Undergraduate, plagiarized essay
  from, 164–166
University:
  foreign, changing grade from, 11–14
  survey about cheating at, 56–58
*Using Relational Coordination to Promote
  Academic Integrity*, 58–61

V
Vargas, Kacy, 95–97
Vendors:
  machine learning models, 39–43
  online proctoring, 26–29
Victimization, 74
Visa cancellation, 167–169

W
Weighing the Options, 135–137

You Mean Students are in Charge?, 63–65
pp, 158–159
e Bones are Good: Laying the Foundation for Faculty, 111–113
re in the Metaverse is Boris' Voice, 36–38
here's Waldo: IP Address Incongruence and Student Surrogacy, 18–24
Whistleblowers, 158–160, 173–175
Wills, Michael S., 39–43
Wilson, Blaire N., 29–32, 46–48, 53–55, 63–65, 75–77, 90–92, 107–111, 139–141, 164–166
Wolf, Joshua, 88–90, 111–113, 116–118, 121–122

Workload:
  of remote teams, 146–148
  student, cheating and, 47
Writing. *See also* Essays
  and artificial intelligence, 36–38
  auto-thesaurus in, 169–171
  capturing similarities in, 50–53
  chemistry lab reports, 43–44
  citation in, 88–90 (*See also* Citation)
  credit as co-senior author, 176–178
  drafts of, 77–79
  plagiarism (*see* Plagiarism)
  reusing work, 45–46
  scaffolding, 127–129
  spinning in, 95–97
  standards for, 23

CPSIA information can be obtained
at www.ICGtesting.com
Printed in the USA
JSHW050251070123
35838JS00009B/582